Yukio Mishima

AFTER THE BANQUET

Translated from the Japanese by
Donald Keene

A BERKLEY MEDALLION BOOK
PUBLISHED BY
BERKLEY PUBLISHING CORPORATION

Copyright © 1963, by Alfred A. Knopf, Inc.

All rights reserved

Published by arrangement with Alfred A. Knopf, Inc.

BERKLEY MEDALLION EDITION,
JUNE, 1971

SBN 425-02011-8

*BERKLEY MEDALLION BOOKS are published by
Berkley Publishing Corporation
200 Madison Avenue
New York, N.Y. 10016*

BERKLEY MEDALLION BOOKS ® TM 757,375

Printed in the United States of America

CONTENTS

CHAPTER

- I : THE SETSUGOAN — 5
- II : THE KAGEN CLUB — 11
- III : MRS. TAMAKI'S OPINION — 20
- IV : THE LEISURED COMPANIONS — 26
- V : KAZU'S INTERPRETATION OF LOVE — 34
- VI : BEFORE THE DEPARTURE — 41
- VII : THE OMIZUTORI CEREMONY IN NARA — 48
- VIII : THE WEDDING — 58
- IX : THE SO-CALLED "NEW LIFE" — 68
- X : IMPORTANT VISITORS — 77
- XI : "THE NEW LIFE"—THE REAL THING — 87
- XII : COLLISION — 105
- XIII : AN OBSTACLE IN THE PATH OF LOVE — 114
- XIV : THE ELECTION AT LAST — 121
- XV : ELECTION DAY — 141
- XVI : ORCHIDS, ORANGES, BEDROOM — 151
- XVII : A GRAVE IN THE EVENING CLOUDS — 160
- XVIII : AFTER THE BANQUET — 174
- XIX : BEFORE THE BANQUET — 189

THIS TRANSLATION IS DEDICATED TO

Paul C. Blum

CHAPTER I

THE SETSUGOAN

The Setsugoan—the After-the-Snow Retreat—stood on high ground in a hilly part of the Koishikawa district of Tokyo. It had fortunately escaped unharmed during the war; nothing had been damaged either in the magnificent garden, a noted example of the Kobori Enshu style covering over a hundred thousand square feet, or in the buildings: a central gate moved here from a certain famous temple in Kyoto, an entrance and visitors' pavilion lifted bodily from some ancient temple of Nara, and a banqueting hall of more recent construction.

At the height of the upheaval caused by the capital levy after the war, the Setsugoan had passed from the hands of its former owner, an industrialist who dabbled as a tea master, to those of a beautiful, vivacious woman. Under her management the Setsugoan quickly developed into a distinguished restaurant.

The proprietress of the Setsugoan was called Kazu Fukuzawa. A streak of rustic simplicity in Kazu's plump, attractive figure, always bursting with energy and enthusiasm, made people with complicated motives who came before her feel ashamed of their complexity. People with drooping spirits, when they saw Kazu, were either considerably heartened or else completely overpowered. Some curious blessing of heaven had joined in one body a man's resolution with a woman's reckless enthusiasm. This combination carried Kazu to heights no man could reach.

Kazu radiated open good nature, and her absolutely

unyielding disposition had assumed a form both simple and beautiful. Ever since she was a child she had preferred to love rather than be loved. Her air of innocent rusticity concealed a considerable determination to have her own way, and various underhanded acts by petty individuals around her had only served to nurture her infinitely direct and outgoing disposition.

Kazu had for many years enjoyed the company of a number of male friends with whom she had no romantic connections. Genki Nagayama, a politician who worked behind the scenes in the Conservative Party, was a comparatively new friend, but he loved Kazu, twenty years his junior, as he might a younger sister. "You won't find many women like her," he would always say. "One of these days she's going to do something sensational. It wouldn't be too much for Kazu if you told her to stand Japan on its head. Any man with her ability would rank as a child of destiny, but the most you can say about Kazu, since she's a woman, is that she's got plenty of natural endowments. When the day comes that a man coaxes some honest-to-goodness love out of her, she'll really explode."

Nagayama's comments did not upset Kazu when they were relayed to her, but a few days later, sitting beside him, she said, "You'll never coax any romance out of me, Genki. I don't respond when a man comes charging at me bursting with confidence. You're clever enough when it comes to sizing up people, but you're no good at persuasion."

"I've no intention of trying to persuade you. If ever I tried courting you, that would be the end of me!" There was malice in the old politician's tone.

The maintenance of the garden of the Setsugoan was all that its popularity demanded. The focal point of the garden, especially at moon-viewing parties, was a pond directly south of what had been the visitors' pavilion of a Nara temple. Trees of an age and grandeur rarely encountered nowadays in Tokyo surrounded the garden, and each pine, chestnut, nettle tree, and oak rose majestically into a blue sky untroubled by the face of any incongruous modern construction. A pair of kites had for years been accustomed to build their nest at the top of one of the trees, a conspicuously tall pine. Every variety of bird visited this garden at its appointed time of year, but nothing could compare to the numbers and din in the migration season, when flocks of birds swooped down from the sky to peck at the nandin fruits or the insects in the broad expanse of lawn.

Every morning Kazu took a stroll through the garden. She never failed to give instructions of one sort or another to the gardener. Sometimes her suggestions were appropriate, but as often they missed the mark. In any case, giving instructions had become part of Kazu's daily routine and her good humor. The head gardener, though an expert at his trade, consequently never dared oppose her.

Kazu walked in her garden. This walk was the sum of her pleasure in being unmarried and the occasion for unhampered reveries. Almost her entire day was spent chatting with her guests or singing for them; she was never alone. Entertaining guests, however familiar a part of her life it had become, never ceased to exhaust her. Kazu's morning promenade was in fact evidence of the serenity of a heart unlikely ever again to fall seriously in love.

Love no longer disturbed her private life . . . This certainty enraptured Kazu, even as she watched the sunlight shine majestically through the haze-enshrouded trees and glitter magically on the green moss of the path ahead. It had been a long time since she and love had parted company. Her last affair was already a distant memory, and she was unshakably convinced that she was proof against all manner of dangerous sentiments.

This morning stroll was the poem of Kazu's security. She was over fifty, but no one seeing this carefully groomed woman, whose complexion and sparkling eyes had lost none of their loveliness, as she sauntered through the huge garden could help but be struck and moved to romantic conjectures. But, as Kazu herself realized better than anyone, for her romantic stories were a thing of the past, her poem was dead. Kazu naturally sensed the latent strength within her, but she was well aware at the same time that this strength had been bent and curbed, and would never cast off its shackles and break loose.

This huge garden and house, deposits in the bank, negotiable securities, powerful and generous customers from the world of finance—these all were adequate guarantees for Kazu's old age. Having achieved this security, it no longer bothered her that people might dislike her or gossip behind her back. Her roots were firmly planted in the society of her choosing, and she could look forward to spending her remaining years comfortably, respected by everyone, devoting herself to refined pursuits, scattering largesse on her travels and in social expenses, eventually tutoring a suitable successor.

At times, when such thoughts crowded her mind, it made her pause in her walk. She would sit on the garden bench and let her eyes wander far down the moss-covered path, taking in the morning sunlight spilling onto the path and the delicate movements of birds alighting.

Here not an echo of the rumbling of streetcars or the blasts of klaxons could reach her. The world had become a still-life picture. How was it possible that emotions which once had flared so brightly could flicker out without a trace? The reasons escaped Kazu. She was at a loss to understand where sensations which had once definitely passed through her body could have gone. The conventional belief that people achieve maturity as they accumulate experiences of every kind seemed to her untrue. She thought it more likely that human beings were no more than blind ditches through which sundry objects flowed, or the stone pavement at a crossroads printed with the tracks of vehicles of every kind which have since passed on. Ditches rot and stone pavement wears away. But once they too were at a crossroads on a festival day.

It had been years since Kazu knew what it meant to be blind. Everything seemed now to have sharp outlines and to be pellucidly clear, like her view of this garden in morning sunlight; not a single point of ambiguity remained in the world. She felt as if even the insides of other people's minds were now transparent before her eyes.

There weren't so many things to be surprised at any more. When she heard that some man had betrayed his friend for money, she thought it likely; when she heard that another man had failed in business because of infatuation for a woman, that seemed likely too. She was sure of one thing at any rate—such disasters would never overtake her.

When people asked Kazu's advice about their love affairs, her suggestions were adroit and to the point. Human psychology was for her divided into some twenty or thirty clearly defined compartments, and however difficult the problem, she could supply an answer to all questions merely by combining the different elements involved. There was nothing more complicated to human life. Kazu's advice was based on a number of precepts and on being in the position to offer accurate advice to anyone at all in her capacity of retired champion. She accordingly (and quite naturally) despised the idea of "progress." Could anyone, however modern he fancied himself, be an exception to rules of passion which have existed from remote antiquity?

"The young people these days," Kazu would often remark, "are doing exactly what young people have always done. Only the clothes are different. Young people get the foolish idea that what is new for them must be new for everybody else too. No matter how unconventional they get, they're just repeating what others before them have done. The only difference is that society doesn't make as much fuss about their antics as it used to, and the young people have to go to bigger and bigger extremes in order to attract attention."

There was nothing new or startling about this pronouncement, but coming from Kazu it had authority.

Kazu, still seated on the bench, took a cigarette from the sleeve of her kimono and enjoyed a quiet puff. The smoke drifted in the morning light and hung in the windless air, bright and heavy as silk. This moment had a savor that a woman with a family would surely never know; it brought the taste of assurance that she could provide herself with a comfortable life. Kazu enjoyed such good health that no matter how heavily she might have drunk the previous night, she could not remember ever having failed to enjoy her morning cigarette.

Kazu could not see it all from where she sat, but the whole landscape of the garden was firmly graven in her mind; she knew it to the last detail as well as she knew the palm of her hand. The tall dusky-green ilex tree that formed the center of the garden, its clusters of glossy, pudgy little leaves, the wild vines twisted about the trees on the hill in back . . . the view from the reception room of the main building, a broad expanse of lawn and an unobtrusive snow-viewing lantern in front, the island in the garden pond with its ancient pagoda and thick growth of bamboo grass: nothing, not the smallest clump of shrubbery, nor the least conspicuous flower, grew in this garden by accident. As she smoked her cigarette Kazu felt as if the garden's exquisite perfection had completely enveloped all her memories. Kazu looked on people and society as she now looked on this garden. And that was not all. She owned it.

CHAPTER II

THE KAGEN CLUB

Kazu received word from a certain cabinet member that the Kagen Club would like to hold its annual meeting at her establishment. The Kagen Club was a kind of association of former ambassadors who were roughly contemporaries and who met once a year on the seventh of November. They had hitherto been unlucky with their meeting places, and the cabinet member, feeling sorry for them, put in a word with Kazu.

"They're a bunch of elegant, retired gentlemen," he said, adding, "All except one, who's never quite retired. I'm sure you've heard of him—old Noguchi, the famous Noguchi who was in the cabinet any number of times before the war. I don't know what's come over him, but a couple of years ago he was elected to the Diet on the Radical ticket, only to get beaten in the next election."

Kazu learned of the club's plans in the midst of a garden party given by the minister, and she was too busy entertaining the guests to listen to more. The garden had been invaded that day by a crowd of foreign men and women. It was as if a flock of birds—not the usual twittering little creatures, but a chattering swarm of oversized, brightly feathered birds, had swooped down on the Setsugoan.

As the seventh of November approached, Kazu began making plans. The most important thing with such guests was to express her respect. The same uncomplimentary jokes and familiar behavior which were likely to amuse men at the height of their powers might wound the pride of men who were once renowned but now living in retirement. Her function as hostess when entertaining such elderly guests would be entirely confined to listening. Later, she would massage them with soft words, and give them the illusion that in this company their former glory had blossomed again.

The menu at the Setsugoan that evening was as follows.

SOUP
White miso with mushrooms and sesame bean curd
RAW FISH
*Thin slices of squid dipped in parsley
and citron vinegar*
CASSEROLE
*Sea trout in a broth of red clams,
sweet peppers, and citron vinegar*
HORS D'OEUVRES
*Thrush broiled in soy, lobster, scallops,
pickled turnips, liquorice-plant shoots*
ENTREE
Duck and bamboo shoots boiled with arrowroot paste
COOKED FISH
*Two baby carps with sea bass
broiled in salt in a citron vinegar sauce*
VEGETABLE DISH
*Chestnut dumplings with fern shoots
and pickled plums*

Kazu wore on this occasion a small-patterned violet-gray kimono with an obi of dark purple dyed in a single band of chrysanthemum flowers in lozenges. A large black pearl was set in her carnelian obi clasp. She had chosen this particular attire with a view to holding in her ample body and giving it greater dignity.

The day of the reunion was warm and clear. Shortly after dark the former foreign minister, Yuken Noguchi, and the former ambassador to Germany, Hisatomo Tamaki, arrived together at the Setsugoan. Noguchi seemed thin and rather unprepossessing alongside the splendidly built Tamaki, but under the silver hair his eyes were clear and alert; a flash in them told Kazu why this unmistakable idealist was the only one of the assembling guests, all former ambassadors, who had not retired.

The party was lively and sociable, but the topics of conversation were confined to the past. The most talkative by far was Tamaki.

The dinner was held in the main reception room of the visitors' pavilion. Tamaki as he ate leaned on a pillar between the black-lacquered bell-shaped window and the magnificently decorated sliding-doors. The paintings on the doors depicted in brilliant colors a pair of peacocks amidst white peonies. By contrast, the background was a landscape executed in monochromes, a curious mélange of styles in the taste of the provincial aristocracy.

Tamaki carried in the waistcoat pocket of his London-tailored suit an old-fashioned watch with a gold chain, a present which his father, also a former ambassador to Germany, had received from Kaiser Wilhelm II. Even in Hitler's Germany this watch had given Tamaki quite a cachet.

Tamaki was a handsome man and a fluent speaker, a diplomat with aristocratic leanings who had formerly prided himself on his knowledge of the harsh realities of life. His present interests, however, quite transcended the contemporary scene. His mind was entirely preoccupied by recollections of the brilliance of chandeliers at long ago receptions where five hundred or a thousand guests had congregated.

"Here's a story that sends cold chills up my spine every time I think of it. This one is really interesting." Tamaki's self-congratulatory introduction would have dampened the enthusiasm of even the most eager listener. "I had never gone for a ride on the Berlin underground in all my time as ambassador, so one day the counselor of the embassy—Matsuyama was his name—dragged me off for the experience. We boarded the train two cars—no, it was more likely three—from the rear. It was fairly crowded when we got on. I happened to look up, when who should I see before me but Goering!"

Tamaki paused at this point to study his listeners'

reaction, but everyone had apparently heard the story dozens of times, and no response was forthcoming. Kazu, stepping into the breach, chimed in, "But he was a very famous man at that time, wasn't he? You don't mean that he was riding on the underground?"

"He was indeed. Goering, who ruled the roost at the time, dressed in shabby workman's clothes, with his arm around a teen-age girl, a real beauty, riding the underground, cool as you please. I rubbed my eyes, wondering if it wasn't a case of mistaken identity, but the harder I looked, the surer I was that it was Goering himself. After all, I was in a positon to know—I saw him at receptions almost every day. I was staggered, I confess, but he didn't so much as bat an eye. The girl must have been a prostitute, but unfortunately that is one subject I'm ignorant of."

"You don't look it," Kazu said, by way of a compliment.

"She was really an attractive girl, but there was something suspiciously coarse about her make-up, the lipstick especially. Goering, nonchalant as you please in his laborer's get-up, was playing with the girl's ear lobe and stroking her back. I looked at Matsuyama standing beside me. His eyes were popping out of his head. Goering and the girl got off two stations later. Matsuyama and I, still on the train, were flabbergasted. For the rest of the day I couldn't get the sight of Goering on the underground out of my head. The following evening Goering gave a reception. Matsuyama and I went up close to him and examined him carefully. There was no doubt about it—he looked exactly the same as the man we had seen the previous day.

"I was unable to restrain my curiosity any longer. I forgot my position as ambassador, and before I knew it I was saying to Goering, 'Yesterday we took a ride on the underground. We wanted to observe how the ordinary people get about. I really think it was a worthwhile experience. I wonder if Your Excellency has ever done the same?'

"At this Goering grinned, but his answer was

profound, "We are always at one with the people and part of the people. I have never felt it necessary therefore to ride on the underground.' " Tamaki gave Goering's reply in succinct German, at once adding a Japanese translation.

There was nothing diplomatic about these former ambassadors despite their solemn appearance; they made not the least pretense of listening to what anyone else said. The former ambassador to Spain, hardly able to wait for Tamaki to finish his story, began to talk about his life as Minister to the Dominican Republic in the beautiful capital of Santo Domingo. The walk along the sea under a palm grove, the superb sunsets over the Caribbean, the dusky skins of the mulatto girls glowing in the sunset . . . The old man was quite carried away by his own painstaking description of these sights, but the eloquent Ambassador Tamaki, broke in again and turned the conversation to his story of meeting Marlene Dietrich when she was still young. For Tamaki stories about unknown beautiful women were of no interest; a world-renowned name, a glittering reputation, was a necessary embellishment to every story.

Kazu felt uncomfortable with all the different foreign words thrown into the conversation, and it annoyed her especially that the punch lines of dirty jokes were invariably delivered in the original language. At the same time, men from the world of diplomacy rarely visited her restaurant, and she was intrigued by the special atmosphere surrounding them. There was no question but that they were all "elegant retired gentlemen," and even if they were poor now, in the past their fingers had known the touch of real luxury. Sadly enough, the memory of those days had stained their fingers forever with a golden powder.

Only Yuken Noguchi seemed different and stood out from the others. His manly face had a straightforward ruggedness it would never lose, and, unlike the others, his attire was utterly devoid of affectation or dandyism. Thick, strikingly long eyebrows jutted above his sharp, clear eyes. His features taken individually were impressive, but they warred with one another, and his lean build accentuated the disharmony. Noguchi did not forget to smile at the appropriate times, but he only rarely joined in the conversation, a sign that he was constantly on guard. Kazu could not help noticing such distinctive features, but what caught her attention especially on this first encounter was the faint smudge which clung like a shadow to the back of Noguchi's collar.

"Just think—a former cabinet minister wearing a shirt like that! Has he no one to look after him, I wonder?" The thought bothered Kazu, and she unobtrusively glanced at the necks of the other guests. The collars that mercilessly pinched the dried-up skins of these elegant old gentlemen all shone a gleaming white.

Noguchi was the only one who did not talk about the past. He had also served as ambassador to various small countries before returning to the Foreign Ministry, but the gaudy life of the diplomatic set lay outside his present interests. His refusal to discuss the past seemed a sign that he alone was still alive.

Ambassador Tamaki began again, this time with the story of a bygone dinner party, a dazzling reception at a palace, where the royalty and nobility of all Europe had gathered under the brilliant chandeliers. The decorations and jewels of all Europe were on display, and the cheeks of the old gentlewomen, wrinkled and spotted like faded white roses, paled in the reflections of the innumerable precious stones.

Next followed stories of opera singers of former days. One ambassador proclaimed the supremacy of Galli-Curci's Mad Scene in *Lucia,* another insisted that Galli-Curci had by that time already passed her peak, and declared that Dal Monte's Lucia, which he had heard, was far superior.

Noguchi, who had scarcely uttered a word, finally spoke. "Why don't we drop all this talk about the old days? We're still young, after all."

Noguchi spoke with a smile, but the surging strength in his tone made the others fall silent.

Kazu was captivated by this one remark. It is the

function of the hostess in such a case to relieve the silence by making some foolish observation or other, but Noguchi's comment hit the mark so precisely, and expressed so perfectly what she herself would have liked to say, that she forgot her duties. She thought, "This gentleman can say beautiful things which are really difficult to say."

Noguchi's comment was all that was necessary for the sparkle to fade instantly from the party; nothing was left now but the black, wet ashes smoldering after water has been dashed on a fire. One old gentleman coughed. His painful gasping after the coughing trailed across the silence of the others. For a moment, as was plain from their faces, everyone thought of the future, of death.

Just then the garden was swept by a wave of bright moonlight. Kazu called the guests' attention to the late moonrise. The liquor had already taken considerable effect, and the old gentlemen, unafraid of the night chill, proposed that the party take a turn around the garden in order to inspect its charms not visible by day. Kazu ordered the maids to fetch paper lanterns. The old man who had been coughing, reluctant to be left behind, bundled himself in a muffler and followed the others out.

The visitors' pavilion had slender pillars, and the railing of the porch projecting into the garden had the delicate construction found in old temples. The moon just emerging over the roof to the east framed the building in heavy shadows, and the maids held up paper lanterns to illuminate the steps going down into the garden.

All went well as long as the party remained on the lawn, but when Tamaki proposed that they walk along the path on the other side of the pond, Kazu regretted having called the guests' attention to the November moon. The five men standing on the lawn looked terribly frail and uncertain.

"It's dangerous. Do watch your step, please," she urged. But the more Kazu cautioned them, the more stubbornly the old men, who disliked being treated as such, insisted on following the path under the trees. The moonlight seemed lovelier than ever through the branches overhead, and anyone who had come as far as the pond with its reflections of the moon could not have resisted the temptation to go round to the other side.

The maids, instinctively aware of Kazu's wishes, bustled about, shining their lanterns on dangerous rocks, stumps, and slippery patches of moss, and carefully pointing them out to the guests. "How chilly the evenings have become!" Kazu remarked, holding her sleeves to her breast. "And today it was so warm." Noguchi was walking beside her, and she could see the puffs of his breath, white under his mustache in the moonlight. He did not choose to follow up her observations.

Kazu, walking at the head of the party in order to lead the way, inadvertently went too fast for those behind, and the lanterns accompanying them bobbed frantically under the trees. The lanterns and the moon reflected charmingly in the pond. The sight affected Kazu more than it did the old gentlemen, and it filled her with a childish excitement. She called in a loud voice across the pond, "It's lovely! Look at the pond, look!"

A smile flickered over Noguchi's lips. "What an incredibly loud voice! You sound like a girl!"

The accident occurred after they had safely completed their turn of the garden and returned to the visitors' pavilion. Kazu had seen to it that a gas stove was burning cheerfully in the dining room, and the old gentlemen, chilled by the night air, gathered around the fire, relaxing in whatever posture they chose. Fruit was served, followed by Japanese cakes and powdered tea. Tamaki had fallen silent, depriving the conversation of much of its liveliness. It was time to be preparing to leave, and Tamaki went to the toilet. When the others were at last ready to get up, they noticed that Tamaki had not yet returned. They decided to wait a while longer. The silence in the room became oppressive. The four old men acted as if their only subject of conversation was one which nobody wished to touch.

The talk turned to a discussion of the health of each. One complained of asthma, another of stomach trouble, the third of low blood pressure. Noguchi, a grave expression on his face, made no attempt to join in the conversation. "I'll go have a look," he said quietly, rising. Kazu, apparently emboldened by his words to get up and investigate, showed him the way, walking quickly down the smoothly polished corridor. Ambassador Tamaki had collapsed in the lavatory.

CHAPTER III

MRS. TAMAKI'S OPINION

Never before in her career as proprietress of the Setsugoan had Kazu been faced with such a situation. She shrieked for help. The maids flocked to her, and she ordered them to summon all the male employees. By this time the other members of the Kagen Club were clustered in the corridor.

Kazu could hear quite close-by Noguchi's calm voice talking to the others. "It's probably a stroke. I hate to bother the restaurant, but I think it best we not move him too much. We'll ask a doctor to come here. Leave everything to me. You all have families. I'm the only one with nothing to tie me down."

It was strange that amidst all this excitement Noguchi's words—"I'm the only one with nothing to tie me down"—should have lingered so vividly in Kazu's mind. Yes, those definitely had been Noguchi's words, and their meaning, like the vibrations of a silver wire, sent a glow of light into Kazu's heart.

Kazu threw herself with utter sincerity into ministering to the stricken man, but all she could clearly remember in her agitation was Noguchi's remark. Not long afterward Mrs. Tamaki rushed in. Kazu felt deeply responsible before her, but even as she was weeping and apologizing for her negligence—and there was absolutely no pretense in this display of her feelings—Noguchi's words continued to echo vividly in her brain.

Noguchi, beside her, reassured Kazu. "You're taking

your responsibilities too seriously. This was Tamaki's first time as a guest here, and you knew nothing about the state of his health. And, after all, it was Tamaki himself who proposed that we go out in the cold for a stroll round the garden."

The stricken man continued to emit loud snores.

Mrs. Tamaki, an attractive middle-aged woman who looked much younger than her years, was stylishly dressed and seemed unruffled in the face of her husband's serious condition. She frowned slightly whenever she caught the sound of samisens from the main banqueting hall, where a party was still in progress. Mrs. Tamaki was exceedingly self-possessed, and when the doctor advised that her husband be left at the Setsugoan for at least a full day, she rejected the suggestion firmly, giving excellent reasons. "It has always been a motto of my husband never to cause others any trouble. If I allow the Setsugoan to be inconvenienced any further, I dread to think how upset my husband will be once he's recovered. After all, this restaurant has many guests, and it isn't as if my husband were a customer of long standing. I can't permit the proprietress to be bothered any further. My husband must be taken to a hospital as soon as possible."

Mrs. Tamaki enumerated the same arguments again and again in her elegant diction, thanking Kazu repeatedly as she did so. Kazu opposed Mrs. Tamaki's decision. "You needn't stand on ceremony," she insisted. "Please leave your husband here until the doctor says it's all right for him to be moved, no matter how long it takes." This touching scene of old-fashioned courtesy, enacted beside the pillow of the snoring patient, was accompanied by interminable expressions of mutual deference. Mrs. Tamaki never for a moment lost her composure, nor did Kazu for her part flag in her undiluted, overpowering solicitude. The heavy-set doctor in the end was utterly exhausted.

The patient had been carried into a little-used detached building. The room was fairly large, but what with the sick man, Noguchi, Mrs. Tamaki, the doctor, the nurse, and Kazu, it presented quite a congested sight. Noguchi, signaling Kazu with his eyes, left the room, and she followed him out into the corridor. Noguchi strode quickly along the corridor ahead of her, walking with such assurance that Kazu, watching him from behind, felt as if this were Noguchi's house and she herself merely a casual visitor.

Noguchi walked straight ahead, quite at random. He crossed over a passageway arched like a humped bridge, continued down the next corridor, then turned to the left. They emerged on an inner garden filled with white chrysanthemums. No flowers grew in the front garden, but the small back garden had flowers all year round.

The two small connecting rooms facing the garden were Kazu's private apartment. The rooms were dark now. A small, unpretentious garden was what Kazu wanted for herself when she was away from her work. The plants and flowers were not laid out in any stiff, orderly pattern, nor were there the usual garden stones and stone basins disposed in the prescribed manner. Kazu wanted a garden like the kind one sees before a bungalow at a summer resort, rows of shells marking the beds of sunplants. The white chrysanthemums had been allowed to grow in disorder, some tall, some short and sparse. At the beginning of autumn the garden had been a tangle of cosmos.

Kazu deliberately refrained from inviting Noguchi into her rooms. Reluctant to display any special friendliness, she did not even inform him that this was where she lived. She offered Noguchi a veranda chair left by the glass doors overlooking the garden.

Noguchi spoke as soon as he was seated. "You're stubborn too. It stops being kindness when you're so insistent."

"But if a guest—even a new one—falls ill while he's here, I can't neglect him."

"Yes, that's what you'd like us to believe. But you're not a child any more. You surely realize that Mrs. Tamaki's reluctance is not mere politeness. You know why she acts that way, don't you?"

"Of course I do." Kazu smiled, the wrinkles gathering a little around her eyes.

"If you understand, it proves you're just as stubborn as she is."

Kazu did not answer.

"Mrs. Tamaki is the kind of women who takes time to make up her face properly even when she hears that her husband's been stricken."

"It's only natural. She's the wife of an ambassador."

"That doesn't necessarily follow." Noguchi broke off the conversation and fell silent. Kazu found the silence extremely agreeable.

Faint sounds of music and voices reached them from the distant main banqueting hall. Kazu felt released at last from her embarrassment and worry over the incident. Noguchi also leaned back in his chair comfortably. He took out a cigarette. Kazu got up to light it.

"Much obliged," Noguchi said. His tone was unemotional, but Kazu was aware of a ring that stemmed from something other than the usual relations between guest and hostess.

Kazu was constitutionally unable to keep from blurting out her happiness as soon as she felt it. "All of a sudden I feel so strangely light-hearted. I'm ashamed when I think of poor Mr. Tamaki. I wonder if the saké is beginning to take effect."

"I suppose so," Noguchi answered indifferently. "I was thinking just now about the vanity of women. I can speak frankly, I hope, to you—Mrs. Tamaki is anxious that her husband die, not in a restaurant, but in a proper hospital bed, even if it means speeding up the end. As for myself, I'd really be sorry to lose an old friend. My own feeling is that I'd like to ask you to let him stay here until he's out of danger . . . But just because I'm his friend I can't fly in the face of his wife's vanity and force my friendship on her."

"That shows you haven't any real feelings for him." Kazu felt she could say anything to Noguchi. "If it was up to me, I'd do as my feelings dictated, no matter what other people might think. That's the way I've always been. Yes, I've always had my way when my feelings were involved."

"I suppose you've let your feelings guide you tonight too." Noguchi's tone was fairly serious. Kazu was in ecstasy at the thought that Noguchi might be jealous of her relations with Tamaki, but she was too honest to keep from adding immediately the quite unnecessary explanation: "Oh, no. I was surprised and I felt responsible, but there's no reason why I should have any special feelings for Mr. Tamaki."

"Then you're simply being obstinate. In that case, Tamaki should be removed as soon as possible." Noguchi, rising from his chair, spoke so coldly and decisively that he left her no ground to stand on. Her illusion was shattered. Kazu's answer, direct and untinged by any emotion, was a fine example of her strong temper.

"Yes, I'll see to that. Exactly as Mrs. Tamaki wishes."

The two returned without another word along the corridor. Not until they were halfway back did Noguchi break the silence. "Tonight, at any rate, once we get him into the hospital, I think I'll go back home for a while. I'll visit him tomorrow about noon. I have nothing else to do."

The guests in the main banqueting hall had apparently all gone home. The sounds of merrymaking had faded away. The night, empty and cavernous now that the banqueting was over, had taken possession of the Setsugoan. Kazu led Noguchi through the banqueting room, the shortest way. The maids clearing up bowed to them. Kazu and Noguchi passed before the two large six-fold gold screens which had served as the background for the evening's entertainment. After the banquet the gold of the screens had settled. They still held a faint glow of warmth, but produced a curiously gloomy atmosphere.

"I didn't appear at this party. Did people say anything when it was breaking up?" Kazu asked one of the maids. The middle-aged, intelligent maid looked up dubiously at Kazu. It was Kazu's practice never to ask questions about business before guests, and Noguchi was obviously a guest.

"No," the maid answered, "everybody was in fine spirits when the party broke up."

Noguchi and Kazu quietly slid open the door of the room where Tamaki lay. Mrs. Tamaki, attending the sick man, looked up sharply at them. Her eyebrows were penciled in an extremely thin line, and the pin holding her black hat in place, slipped somewhat out of place, flickered in the light from the hallway.

CHAPTER IV

THE LEISURED COMPANIONS

Ambassador Tamaki was soon afterward moved to the university hospital. When Kazu went to visit him about noon the following day, she was informed that he was still in a coma. She sent to Tamaki's room the basket of fruit she had brought, then withdrew to a chair some distance down the corridor, where she waited for Noguchi. Kazu knew from her impatience—she thought Noguchi would never arrive—that she must be fond of him.

Kazu, now that she thought of it, realized that for all her headstrong temperament, she had never loved a man younger than herself. A young man has such a surplus of spiritual and physical gifts that he is likely to be cocksure of himself, particularly when dealing with an older woman, and there is no telling how swelled up with self-importance he may become. Besides, Kazu felt a physical repugnance for youth. A woman is more keenly aware than a man of the shocking disharmony between a young man's spiritual and physical qualities, and Kazu had never met a young man who wore his youth well. She was moreover repelled by the sleekness of a young man's skin.

Kazu mulled endlessly over such matters as she waited in the gloomy, dimly lit hospital corridor. Tamaki's room was easily distinguishable at the end of the long corridor by the baskets of flowers protruding from the door. Kazu was suddenly aware of many dogs barking, and looked out the window. She could see under the cold overcast sky a large area enclosed in wire netting, a pen for the stray dogs used in laboratory experiments. An immense number of roughly built kennels, absolutely devoid of any semblance of order, was jammed together. Some were built like chicken coops; others were the usual watchdog kennels. No two kennels stood at the same angle: some leaned precariously, others had tumbled over on one side, no doubt tugged over by the dogs chained to them. The dogs were no less disparate: some were mangy and emaciated looking, but others were healthy and well-fed. All were simultaneously howling pitifully, as if appealing for sympathy.

The hospital employees were apparently hardened to the dogs' howling, and no one even paused as he went by the wire netting. Beyond the enclosure an old three-storied building—a laboratory—bared a row of small, gloomy windows. The panes reflecting the cloudy sky seemed like sluggish eyes which had lost all sense of curiosity.

Kazu's heart swelled with a warm rush of sympathy as she listened to the pathetic howling of the dogs. The intensity of her agitation came as quite a surprise even to herself. "Those poor dogs! Those poor dogs!" She was in tears. She tried desperately to think if there were not some way of saving them. This helped to relieve the tedium of waiting.

Noguchi arrived to find Kazu weeping. One look at her face and he demanded, "Is he dead?" Kazu quickly reassured him, but in her embarrassment she had no chance to explain her tears.

Noguchi blurted out the childish, nonsensical question. "Are you waiting for someone?"

"No," Kazu answered distinctly. A smile at last rose to her well-rounded cheeks.

"That's fine," Noguchi said. "It won't take me long to get through with the visit. Please wait here for me. I have nothing to do, and I imagine that you're free during the day. People of leisure—that's what we both are. Let's go downtown and have lunch together."

The clouds broke up as they were walking down the

gently sloping stone pavement behind the university hospital, and a pale, watery sunlight fell over the landscape.

Kazu had kept a car waiting, but she sent it back when Noguchi suggested that they walk.

Noguchi's voice when he proposed the walk, making a point of deliberately sending back the car, had a ring of moral conviction. It gave Kazu the impression that her extravagance was being indirectly criticized. Kazu was later to have numerous occasions to correct his initial impression, but Noguchi's appearance and manner of speech were always so exceedingly dignified that his least whim or caprice seemed a kind of moral judgment.

They started to cross the street on their way toward Ikenohata Park. The road swarmed with cars weaving in and out. Kazu was confident she could easily get to the other side, but Noguchi, surprisingly cautious, showed no sign of venturing across. When Kazu started to make a break for it, he restrained her with a "Not yet!" and she was obliged to let a good opportunity slip. The opening in the traffic through which they surely could have crossed was immediately swallowed up by the flow of on-coming vehicles, their windshields reflecting in the winter sun. Kazu finally lost patience. "Now—now's our chance," she cried. Instantly she caught Noguchi's hand firmly in hers and began to run.

Kazu still clung to Noguchi's hand even after they had reached the other side. The hand was exceedingly desiccated and thin, rather like a botanical specimen, but when Kazu seemed reluctant to let go, Noguchi gradually, almost furtively, withdrew it. Kazu had been quite unconscious of still holding his hand, but Noguchi's gingerly manner of disengaging it made her aware of her indiscretion. His hand escaped like a peevish child twisting its body from the arms of an adult.

Kazu inadvertently glanced at Noguchi's face. The sharp eyes under the severe eyebrows were quite unperturbed, as if nothing had happened.

They went up to the pond in the park and started clockwise on the path around it. The faint but bitterly cold wind blowing over the pond shook wrinkles over the surface. The blue and cloud of the winter sky mingled in the trembling water, the sparkling blue rifts stretching to the water's edge at the opposite shore. Five or six boats were out on the pond.

The embankment was carpeted with slender willow leaves, some yellow but others mottled with light green; the fallen leaves looked much fresher than the dusty shrubbery around them, flecked with scraps of paper.

A group of middle-school students out for running practice in white gym suits approached from the opposite direction. They seemed to have run once or twice around the pond already, and their youthful, delicate brows contracted with painful breathing recalled the Asura statue in the Kofukuji Temple. The boys ran past the two strollers, not looking to either side, leaving behind the sound of their sneakers lightly striking the ground. One boy had a pink towel tied around his neck, and it could still be seen in the distance under the row of barren trees long after he had gone by.

Noguchi seemed unable to resist calling Kazu's attention to the close to half a century separating him from these youngsters. "They're wonderful—kids are certainly wonderful. A friend of mine's a boy scout leader. I used to think that was a silly way to spend his time, but I see now why he'd want to throw himself into that kind of work."

"Yes," Kazu responded, "it's marvelous how unsophisticated children are." But such innocence seemed so remote and unattainable to Kazu that it arose no envy. She felt moreover that Noguchi's observations had been excessively plain and uninspired.

They watched the boys run around the pond into the distance, casting their reflections in the water. Beyond the pond stretched the melancholy clusters of buildings at Ueno Hirokoji. Two tomato-colored ad balloons rose in a sky hazy with soot.

Kazu suddenly noticed how worn the cuffs of Noguchi's overcoat were. Each discovery she made about him seemed to come as a criticism of herself. She felt that this at any rate was one discovery she could do nothing about, that it rejected any meddling on her part from the outset.

Noguchi, surprisingly sensitive to her glance, asked, "Is this what you're looking at? I had this overcoat made in London in 1928. As long as your heart is young, the older your clothes the better. Don't you agree?"

Noguchi and Kazu cut across Benten Island, surrounded now by withered lotus leaves, and passed through the entrance of the Gojo Tenjin Shrine to start the climb up Ueno Hill. The pale blue of the winter sky looked like a glass painting behind the delicate shadow pictures of the barren trees. They were still looking up at the sky when they reached the old-fashioned entrance of the Seiyoken Restaurant. The grill room had few guests at lunch time.

Noguchi ordered the table d'hôte meal, and Kazu did the same. Directly before their windowside table they could see an old temple belltower. Kazu, delighted that the room was so comfortably heated, said with undisguised relief, "That was certainly a cold walk!"

Kazu's mind however had colored that chilly stroll with tints she had never known in her normal busy routine of entertaining customers. The walk had given her a slight surprise. Kazu seldom bothered to analyze her actions at any given moment, preferring to collect and try to understand her thoughts later on. She might, for example, suddenly burst into tears while talking with someone. The tears would flow even though she did not at the time understand what prompted them, her own emotions unperceived by herself.

Even after Kazu commented on how cold it had been, Noguchi did not apologize for having obliged her to walk. Kazu therefore felt impelled to explain in minute detail how much she had enjoyed the walk despite the cold. Finally, after Kazu had gone on at great length, Noguchi broke in, profiting by the appearance of the first course. "I'm glad," he laconically remarked. Noguchi's face remained impassive even as he said this, but somehow he seemed happy.

This was Kazu's first encounter with such a man. Kazu always talked more than her customers, some of whom were extremely close-mouthed, but Noguchi seemed to be manipulating Kazu with his silences. She could not understand how this old man, so simple in all his tastes, could possess such strength.

There was a pause in the conversation and Kazu looked around her at the stuffed bird-of-paradise in a glass case, the sober-colored material of the curtains, the plaque inscribed in Chinese characters "A Hall Filled With Splendid Guests," an engraving of the old warship *Ise* built at the Kawasaki Shipyard. The picture, executed in the copperplate techniques of the early nineteenth century, showed the battleship *Ise* plowing through the fine lines of the waves, its red hull visible like a petticoat under the waterline. This turn-of-the-century Western-style restaurant, the former cabinet minister eating lunch in his old-fashioned English clothes—in fact, everything around her went so well together that Kazu, who prized the vitality of whatever was currently at the height of its popularity, was somehow irritated.

Noguchi began to speak. "Diplomacy boils down to knowing how to size up people. That's one art I think I've acquired in the course of my long life. My deceased wife was a splendid woman, and I knew it the first time I laid eyes on her. One look was enough for me to decide. But I'm no fortuneteller. I couldn't predict how long she'd live. My wife took sick and died just after the war ended. We hadn't any children, so I'm completely alone now . . . Oh—when there's only a little soup left in your plate you should always tilt it away from you and then put your spoon in. That's right, like this."

Kazu was quite taken aback, but she meekly followed Noguchi's instructions. No man had ever before corrected her manner of eating Western food.

"It won't be till next February," Noguchi continued, paying no attention to the expression on Kazu's face, "but I've been invited by friends to see the Omizutori Ceremony in Nara, and I think I'll go. In all these years I've never once seen the Omizutori. How about you?"

"I've never gone either. I've been invited any number of times, but somehow . . ."

"What do you say—I'm sure you're busy, but how about coming with me?"

"Yes," Kazu answered instantly.

The appointment was still three or four months in the future, but hardly was the word "Yes" out of Kazu's mouth than her spirits soared, and wild fantasies took wing. Her face, glowing from the heat of the room she had entered from the cold, now colored with a rush of blood she could not conceal.

"You've got something like a fire inside you," Noguchi said, manipulating his delicately engraved fish knife. He seemed most satisfied when with full confidence he could foist his observations on others.

"A fire?" Kazu was enchanted to be described in such terms. "A fire?" she repeated. "What does that mean, I wonder? People are always teasing me by saying I'm like a ball of fire, though I don't think so myself."

"I didn't say it to tease you." Noguchi's words had an acidulous ring. Kazu fell silent.

The interrupted conversation was taken up again, Noguchi's subject this time being orchids. Kazu, completely uninformed on this topic, had no choice but to listen in silence as the old man sitting before her paraded his useless knowledge like an adolescent. She could visualize Noguchi dozens of years ago proudly displaying his erudition to some girl he was fond of.

"Do you see those orchids over there? Do you know what they're called?"

Kazu turned her head and looked behind her at a potted plant on a stand. It failed to interest her in the least, and she turned back, hardly giving it a glance. "I don't know," she answered. Her reply came much too quickly.

"They're dendrobiums," Noguchi said in a tone of faint displeasure.

Kazu was thereupon obliged to turn again and examine the flowers more attentively. They were hot-house orchids—not a particularly striking variety—in a small emerald-colored pot on a stand. A cluster of demure little blossoms daubed with crimson hovered over a stalk bare as a horsetail. The intricate shapes, suggesting orchids twisted of paper, looked all the more artificial in the absence of even a breeze to stir them. The more intently Kazu looked at the dark crimson centers of the flowers, the more insolent, the more offensive they seemed, quite unbecoming to this calm winter afternoon.

CHAPTER V

KAZU'S INTERPRETATION OF LOVE

Kazu was afraid after she left Noguchi that afternoon and returned to the Setsugoan that her lunchtime exhilaration might carry over unaltered into her professional working hours. She was pleased above all that someone had shown a special interest in her. This happiness made her realize for the first time how lonely she had been.

She had not felt especially agitated while she was actually with Noguchi, but no sooner did she say goodbye than a whirlwind of varying emotions swirled up inside her. First of all she surrendered herself to visions of keeping Noguchi supplied with clean, freshly laundered shirts and newly made suits of clothes. But Kazu's involvement in this matter hinged on Noguchi's sentiments toward her. Unless she could be sure of them, there was no question of any helpful intervention on her part. Kazu was astonished that uncertainty should have cropped up again in her life, that she should be faced with the predicament of being ignorant of what another person might be thinking. This was not only strange but extremely upsetting.

Kazu tried to think why Noguchi should dress himself in such shabby—if good quality—clothes, and this in turn started her on agonized conjectures about his income. He undoubtedly lived on a pension, and his income could hardly be adequate. For a man who had formerly served in the cabinet, these were certainly sadly reduced circumstances. That night, even as she was busy entertaining her customers, Kazu's mind kept reverting to this subject. She wondered if there weren't some way she could safely inquire into the actual amount of his pension.

As luck would have it, when she appeared in the private room where some officials were having a dinner party, they happened to be talking about what they would do when they reached the retiring age. This gave Kazu the chance to ask quite casually, "If ever the government should start supervising restaurants, I'm sure that the first thing they'd do is to retire old women like myself. But I wouldn't mind. It'd be much nicer living on a pension with nothing to do than staying in a hard business like this one. How much of a pension do you suppose they'd give me?"

"Well, a woman like you would rank on a par with a cabinet minister. Around thirty thousand a month, I suppose."

"Oh, would I really get that much?" Kazu's question had such a transparently false ring that the others laughed.

That evening, alone in her small room, Kazu lay sleepless, her head filled with fantasies of every kind. Kazu's private quarters were, by the standards of the rest of the Setsugoan, extraordinarily shabby and bare. A telephone on a low table stood by her pillow, and around it were disorderly piles of leafed-through magazines. The room contained not one object remotely resembling a work of art; even the tokonoma was cluttered with stacks of little drawers. When Kazu lay down among the bedding that took up the whole room, she felt as if she were her own master at last.

She knew now that his income was thirty thousand yen a month. If that was the case, taking her to lunch today meant quite an extravagance for him. The thought made her more grateful than ever for his kindness. Having at last some concrete materials to work with, her imagination really took flight. She meditated on Noguchi's former position, his present poverty, his resolute attitude in face of adversity. For Kazu, whose daily work was conducted entirely with men at the height of their fortunes, these attributes were stuff of romantic dreams.

The following morning Kazu's eye was caught by an article in the corner of the newspaper that made her cancel her normal stroll in the garden. It reported the death of Tamaki, who had breathed his last at the hospital the night before at ten o'clock. The funeral, it was stated, would be held at the Tsukiji Honganji temple in two days' time. Kazu, anxious to pay a condolence call as soon as possible, went so far as to desist, remembering Mrs. Tamaki's attitude the night of her husband's accident. She spent the next two days waiting and being patient, a process which lit fires in the heart of this passionate woman.

Noguchi ought to have informed Kazu immediately of Tamaki's death, regardless of whether an article had or had not appeared in the newspaper. His telephone call would have served as an index of his affection, or at least of his friendship. But no word came from Noguchi. Every time the telephone rang Kazu, suddenly timid as a little girl, looked faint with terror. She was afraid that the telephone call this time was from Noguchi, telling of the death of his closest friend, and that she would be unable to hide the joy in her voice when she answered him.

Kazu had never waited so impatiently for a funeral service. She had considered the beauty parlor on the previous day, but finally decided to postpone her visit until the morning of the ceremony. Kazu's morning promenade on the day before the funeral made the gardeners stare in astonishment. She failed to greet or even scold them that morning, but instead made a hasty tour round the garden, her eyes fixed on the ground. This had never happened before, and when the proprietress of the Setsugoan embarked on her second tour of the garden, she looked positively demented. The old gardener, who had worked at the Setsugoan since the time of the former owner, said she reminded him of a witch riding on a broomstick.

No telephone call came from Noguchi even on the night before the service. Kazu experienced something akin to a sense of defeat. But the taste of defeat aroused in Kazu all the more intense feelings. It never occurred to her that Noguchi might be so busy with the arrangements for his friend's funeral that he would not have time to get in touch with her. She did not consider any such comforting possibilities. She burned with a single thought—she had been abandoned.

The night before, guided by a thirst for revenge —though she could not be sure whether against Noguchi or Mrs. Tamaki—Kazu had made up a packet of 100,000 yen as her contribution to the funeral expenses. She thought, "It's over three times what he and his friends get for their pensions." She felt as if her only way to vent her feelings was to make such a huge donation, though neither social obligation nor past favors required it.

The services took place on a mild, sunny day, typical of early winter. Even the wind was gentle. Kazu, foregoing her customary stroll, devoted an inordinate length of time to getting into her mourning attire, after which she drove to a beauty parlor on the Ginza.

Kazu watched through the car windows struck by the winter sunlight how the young people walked along the street. She straightened the front of her formal kimono, and directed a knowing and intent look at the young people. They seemed to her exactly like transparencies: their sentiments, ambitions, little tricks, tears, and laughter were all absolutely apparent.

At one corner four university students—two boys and two girls—ran into one another and lifted their hands in exaggerated, un-Japanese gestures of greeting. One of the boys, dressed in a regulation student's uniform and cap, put his hand on a girl's shoulder and let it rest there. The girl wore a half-length coat of some downy, pink material. Apparently unaware of the boy's hand on her shoulder, she absent-mindedly turned her eyes, half-shut in the springlike sunlight, toward the street.

The traffic light flashed green and Kazu's car lurched forward. At that instant she saw an extraordinary sight: the girl in the pink coat suddenly snatched off the student's cap and threw it into the roadway. Kazu instinctively looked out the rear window of the car to see what became of the cap, and was just in time to observe it being crushed by an oncoming vehicle. She also had a glimpse of the student on the other side of the street, stamping his feet in rage.

The driver had followed the whole incident out of the corner of his eye. "The girls these days—you simply can't tell what they'll do next, you simply can't. What made her do such a thing? Imagine!" Kazu could tell from behind that the driver's face had settled into a grim smile.

The lady in mourning replied, "It was just a foolish prank." But, curiously enough, her heart was pounding, captivated by the girl's brash gesture of throwing the boy's cap under the wheels of a car. The act was utterly meaningless. But it had produced an oddly powerful impression on Kazu and everything, down to the student's mussed hair when his cap was torn off, had instantly registered.

This episode lingered in Kazu's mind as her hair was being carefully set at the beauty parlor, a process for which she had allowed ample time. She normally became cheerful and talkative while at the beauty parlor, but today she found little to say. Her face reflected in the mirror was well-rounded and attractive, but the beautician's usual words of flattery were untrue: the face was definitely not young.

The funeral service at the Tsukiji Honganji Temple was fairly elaborate. The line of mourners filed past the wreaths. Kazu joined the line after handing to the receptionist her packet of 100,000 yen. She noticed two or three customers of the Setsugoan and nodded to them deferentially. Incense rose in the early winter sunlight with a refreshing fragrance. Most of the mourners were old men, the one directly in front of Kazu giving off a mechanical noise caused by the incessant clattering of his false teeth.

As the line edged forward it occurred to Kazu that the moment was drawing near when she would see Noguchi, and the thought so unsettled her that she could not keep her mind on anything. Soon afterward the bereaved Mrs. Tamaki came into sight. Her eyes looked forbidding rather than sad, and her gaze, when she lifted her head between deep, polite bows, always seemed to revert to the same fixed point in space, as if it had been jerked back there by a string.

At last Kazu spied Noguchi. He wore a suit of too tightly fitting formal clothes, a piece of black crepe wrapped around the arm. His chin was raised a little, and his face maintained a supreme impassivity.

After all the mourners had offered incense Kazu went up to Noguchi and looked squarely into his eyes. He did not so much as blink; he looked at Kazu with no trace of emotion and respectfully inclined his head.

It cannot be said that these moments at the incense-offering were entirely a disappointment. By a truly absurd process of reasoning Kazu persuaded herself the instant she encountered Noguchi's expressionless eyes that she was in love with him.

Immediately on returning to the Setsugoan, Kazu sat down with a brush and old-fashioned Japanese paper, and wrote the following letter.

Dear Mr. Noguchi,

I had only a glimpse of you today, but I was pleased to see you looking so well. I shall never forget the lunch to which you so kindly invited me the other day, nor the walk around the pond before it. It has been a long time since I have enjoyed such delightful hospitality. You may wonder perhaps if this is merely the joy that someone who normally entertains other people experiences when she herself for a change is entertained, but I should like very much for you to know how happy your thoughtfulness made me.

I have, however, one thing to reproach you for. I read in the newspaper about the death of Mr. Tamaki, and was shocked to learn of it, but at the same time I was unable to understand why you failed to telephone me even once. If you will permit me to express myself frankly, you can hardly imagine how impatiently I have been waiting until this day for the sound of your voice. If you had vouchsafed me even one word, to let me know what had happened, it would have served also to show that you had been thinking of me. I cannot tell you how much your silence disappointed me.

It is not my intent to bore you with tedious complaints, and I hope you will please dismiss this letter as merely an outpouring of impatience from a heart excessively attached to you. I can hardly wait to see you again. It is my reason for living.

Kazu

The next day Kazu, present because of social obligations at a dance recital given by some pupils, burst into tears at the opening refrain of *Yasuna*, "Love, oh love, leave me not in mid-air, love."

A little before noon on the day after, she had a telephone call from Noguchi. He spoke quite casually and made not the slightest allusion to the matter about which he had been reprimanded in Kazu's letter. His voice on the telephone was solemnity itself and completely devoid of humor, but the conversation, though broken by pauses, continued for quite a long time. They promised to meet again. Finally Kazu, unable to restrain herself any longer, asked with a note of asperity, "Why didn't you yourself let me know what had happened?"

Noguchi was silent at the other end of the line, then answered indistinctly with a muffled, embarrassed laugh, "Well, as a matter of fact, there wasn't any reason. It seemed like a lot of bother, that's all."

Kazu could hardly believe her ears. "A lot of bother"—these were clearly the words of an old man.

CHAPTER VI

BEFORE THE DEPARTURE

After this telephone call they met frequently. Kazu even visited Noguchi's house. Noguchi lived by himself in an old house in the Shiina section. Kazu was relieved to discover that the maid looking after him was middle-aged and ugly. In no time at all Kazu was busying herself with various details of Noguchi's private life. She saw to it that a complete New Year dinner was delivered to him from the Setsugoan.

The shelves of Noguchi's study were crowded with books in European languages. Kazu, unable to read even the titles, was awe-struck. Noguchi, well aware of the effect his books would exert on her, had arranged when Kazu visited him that they meet in his study. Kazu artlessly inquired as she looked around at the bookshelves lining the walls, "Have you read them all?"

"Yes, almost all."

"I'm sure some of them are pretty spicy."

"No, there's not one like that."

This declaration genuinely astonished Kazu. A world formed by the intellect and composed of exclusively intellectual elements lay outside her comprehension. Her common sense told her that everything must have its other side. But what continually amazed her in Noguchi was that he was one man without another side: he seemed to have no other face but the one he showed her. Kazu, of course, as a matter of principle disbelieved in the existence of such people. But for all her disbelief, a kind of ideal image, tantalizingly incomplete, was gradually taking shape around Noguchi. His stilted behavior had acquired an aura, indescribably mysterious and intriguing.

Kazu discovered on further acquaintance with Noguchi that the world had almost forgotten his existence. She marveled that Noguchi should not in the least be affected by this neglect. She was totally uninterested in the radical political views which Noguchi now held, but she sensed a disharmony which must some day be resolved between the newness of his ideas and the oblivion of the world. How could this life-in-death go together with vigorous new ideas? Even after Noguchi's second defeat for re-election to the Diet, his name continued to be listed as an adviser of the Radical Party, but the party never sent a car for him when he attended a meeting, and he was obliged to hang on to a leather strap on the streetcar. Kazu, learning this, felt righteous indignation.

Each time Kazu visited Noguchi's house she found something new to distress her in the same way that on first acquaintance she had been upset by the stains on Noguchi's shirt or his frayed cuffs. Now she noticed the sadly asymmetrical front door, or the peeling, dusty paint of the wooden, Western-style house, or the liverwort sprouting inside the gate, or the bell at the entrance left out of order. Kazu was still not at liberty to make repairs as she pleased, and Noguchi was disinclined to permit more than a certain degree of favors from Kazu. His attitude was reserved, but it stimulated Kazu to seek greater intimacy.

In January, at Kazu's suggestion, they went to the Kabuki Theater. Kazu wept freely at the sad moments, not missing a one, but Noguchi sat impassively through the whole performance. "What makes you cry when you see such a silly play?" he asked with genuine curiosity as they stood in the foyer during the intermission.

"There's no particular reason. The tears just come naturally."

"Your naturally interests me. Try to explain more exactly what you mean." Noguchi teased Kazu in solemn tones as if she were a little girl. Noguchi had not the least intention of playing the fox with her, but Kazu felt at such times as if he were genuinely making fun of her, and she was afraid.

That day Noguchi lost his Dunhill lighter in the theater. His consternation when he discovered that the lighter was missing was quite astonishing: all the dignity and calm of a moment before melted away. It was in the middle of the second play of the evening that he noticed the lighter was gone, and he half rose out of his seat to search every pocket for it. The expression on his face as he muttered, "Not here, not here either," bore no resemblance to the usual Noguchi.

"What's the matter?" Kazu asked, but he did not deign an answer. Noguchi finally bent over and thrust his head under the seat. A thought crossed his mind while he was searching, and he said to himself in a fairly loud voice, "The foyer. That's it. I'm sure I dropped it in the foyer."

The spectators around him turned in his direction with frowns and disapproving clucks. Kazu, leading the way, got up and Noguchi followed her out. Once they were out in the foyer, Kazu asked, "Could you please tell me what you lost?" This time she was the calm one.

"My Dunhill lighter. I'll never in the world find one of the old ones in Japan now if I try to replace it."

"Over there is where we were talking during the intermission, isn't it?"

"That's right. It was over there."

Noguchi was virtually gasping, and Kazu felt sorry for him. They went to the spot where they had stood, but nothing was lying on the bright carpet. The attendant at the reception desk, a middle-aged woman in uniform who apparently had time on her hands during the performance, came up and asked, "I wonder if this is what you are looking for?" The object she held forth was unmistakably Noguchi's lighter.

Kazu was to remember long afterward the look of unconcealed joy on Noguchi's face when he saw the lighter, and she would often tease him, "I wish you'd show that expression not only to lighters but to human beings too." But such incidents did not in the least daunt Kazu. Her eyes were free of prejudice, and she saw only Noguchi's childish, simple-minded attachment to his possession.

There were other similar incidents. Noguchi had said at the meeting of the Kagen Club, "Why don't we drop all this talk about the old days? We're still young, after all," and that in fact expressed his attitude toward reminiscences over bygone glories, but when it came to articles belonging to the past, his attachment was extreme. As Kazu got to know Noguchi better, she often noticed him take out an old pocket comb and tidy his silver hair. When she asked him about the comb, it proved to be one he had used for thirty years. When Noguchi was young his hair had been so thick and unruly that the teeth of any ordinary comb were quickly broken. He had had this one specially made for him, a strong comb of boxwood.

Noguchi's tenacious attachment to old possessions could not be laid simply to stinginess or poverty. By way of protest against the superficial elegance created by the relentless pursuit of novelty under an American-style consumer economy, Noguchi stubbornly maintained the English-style elegance of clinging to old customs. The Confucian spirit of frugality went well with these aristocratic tastes. Kazu had difficulty in understanding Noguchi's brand of dandyism which exaggerated its unconcern with fashion.

Kazu, out for the morning promenade that she never missed even in the dead of winter, would wonder as she crushed underfoot the sparkling ice needles, which she liked better, which attracted her more in Noguchi, his aristocratic career as a former cabinet minister, or his present faith in radical ideas. His career had a glittering brilliance which readily appealed to the common run of men; his ideas, though she did not understand them, made her aware of something living and directed toward the future. Kazu had come to think of these two aspects of Noguchi as rather like complementary physical features, and, put as a question of preference, it was like being asked which she preferred, his sharp nose or his prominent ears?

Their love progressed with extreme deliberation. The first time they kissed was when Kazu paid Noguchi a New Year's call at his house. Kazu wore a kimono of celadon-colored silk dyed with vignettes of white bamboo leaves, silver gabions, and dark green dwarf pines. Her sash was embroidered with a large lobster in vermilion and gold on a silver gray ground. She left her mink coat in the car before going in.

Noguchi's gate was bolted, even on New Year's day, and the house looked deserted. But Kazu knew that the broken bell had at last been repaired. In the course of several visits she had become aware that Noguchi's maid, who would appear only after keeping Kazu waiting a long time, looked at her with an expression akin to contempt. Once when Kazu was present Noguchi had asked the maid to fetch from the shelf a book written in German, giving the title in the original. The maid had unfalteringly repeated the German title and, running her eyes over the shelves, immediately picked out the book. Ever since then Kazu had hated the woman.

In this quiet neighborhood removed from the bustle of the main thoroughfares, the only sounds that Kazu could hear as she waited at the door were the clear, dry, distant echoes of children playing at the New Year's sport of battledore and shuttlecock. She always felt humiliated before the driver every time she got out of her car, pressed the bell at Noguchi's gate, and then was kept waiting an eternity. The only sign of New Year at this house was the symbolic branch of pine at the gate, diagonally lit now by the clear winter sunlight.

Kazu stared down the deserted street before the gate. The sunlight brought into bold relief the complicated unevenness of the paving with its broken patches. Shadows of trees and of telegraph poles fell on the road. The black and somehow attractive thawed earth exposed in one place shone where a broad tire track was imprinted on it.

Kazu strained to catch the tap of the battledore and shuttlecock. The children seemed to be playing in a nearby garden, but she could not see them, nor were there laughing voices. The sounds stopped. Ah, Kazu thought, the shuttlecock has fallen. A while later a steady tap-tap told her that the shuttlecock was again bounding back and forth. Then the sound stopped again . . . During the irritating, repeated breaks, Kazu visualized the brightly colored shuttlecock lying in the thawed black mud. Suddenly these intermittent sounds coming from an invisible garden behind a wall suggested to Kazu some sinister game played in stealth where no one could see.

She heard the sounds of geta approaching the side entrance. Kazu braced herself, tense at the thought she would have to encounter Noguchi's disagreeable servant. The gate opened. Noguchi himself came out to greet her, and Kazu blushed at this unexpected surprise.

Noguchi was dressed in formal Japanese clothes. "I gave the maid the day off," he explained. "I'm alone today."

"Happy New Year! Oh, you certainly look impressive in Japanese clothes!"

But even as Kazu stepped through the side gate Noguchi's immaculate attire aroused a sudden flare-up of jealousy. Who had helped him to dress? The thought upset her so much that by the time they were crossing the hall into the living room she was quite out of sorts.

Noguchi made it a practice never to take any notice when Kazu was in a bad temper. He lifted with his own hands a container of the traditional spiced saké and offered some to Kazu. Resentful at having to start the New Year with unpleasant feelings, Kazu as usual gave vent to her emotions.

Noguchi responded, "Don't be foolish. The maid helped me to dress. She doesn't look after my Western clothes as well as she might, but when it comes to kimonos she's on her mettle."

"If you care at all about me, please dismiss that maid. I can find you any number who'll be more attentive. If you don't dismiss her . . ." Kazu broke off and burst into tears. "Even when I'm at home I'm so worried I have trouble sleeping at night."

Noguchi opposed her with his silence. He was counting the jasper-like fruit on a plant in his garden. He listened a while to Kazu's grievances; then, as if he had just remembered it, picked up the spiced saké container again. Kazu, her hands covered by a handkerchief soaked with her tears, took the large cup he pressed on her, only abruptly to fling it on the tatami. She wept, her head pressed against the stiff silk of Noguchi's hakama at the knee. She was careful at the same time to spread the dry part of the handkerchief against the hakama so that the silk would not become soiled.

Noguchi's hand quietly stroked the back of her obi. As he did so Kazu knew for a certainty that her smooth-skinned back, its rich, white resilience discernible through the pulled-back collar of her kimono, had caught Noguchi's eye. Kazu recognized in the gentle, absent-minded movements of Noguchi's hand something like a familiar melody. It was afterward that they first kissed.

CHAPTER VII

THE OMIZUTORI CEREMONY IN NARA

Noguchi had a long-standing engagement to go with Kazu to Nara to see the Omizutori ceremony, but at the same time he was to be the guest of a friend, a newspaper executive. Naturally enough, all the arrangements of the journey were made by the newspaper. Besides Noguchi the party included an octogenarian journalist, an industrialist, and an aged financial columnist. Kazu could not understand when she learned the details why Noguchi should have invited her on what seemed a semi-official excursion.

It was highly improbable that Noguchi, who always distinguished between public and private matters, would bring Kazu along on the same invitation without telling the others. But if they were to travel at his expense, it would be better for the two of them to go somewhere by themselves. There was no reason why they must take a trip on which they would be so conspicuous. It was clear to Kazu from the reports of people who had attended the Omizutori ceremony that even if she and Noguchi made their way to Nara independently of the newspaper party, they would certainly run into the others that night at the Nigatsu Hall.

On top of everything else, Kazu was uneasy about the strain the trip would cause on Noguchi's finances. She also disliked the prospect of feeling small before his distinguished friends. Kazu felt no hesitation in dealing with the most influential men in the country in her capacity as restaurant proprietress, but she disliked being obliged in her private capacity to talk to such people professionally.

Kazu could only make various conjectures. She was irritated with Noguchi for not furnishing her with an explanation. She finally became depressed about the whole thing, and went to visit Noguchi with an envelope containing 200,000 yen. She intended to offer it to him for the expenses of the journey.

Kazu was accustomed to seeing famous politicians calmly accept presents of cash. She had in the past been touched for gifts of one hundred thousand, two hundred thousand, and even a million yen by Genki Nagayama, who needed the money for his personal expenses. But with Noguchi it was different. The money became the occasion for their first quarrel. She discovered that Noguchi looked on the forthcoming journey in truly uncomplicated terms. "All I need pay is your railway ticket and hotel room. I was invited from the start and my expenses are taken care of. When I told the others I was taking the proprietress of the Setsugoan with me, everybody was delighted. The newspaper people offered to invite you too, but I insisted on paying for your share. Doesn't that make sense to you?"

"But the way I see it, this is our first trip together and I'd like to go to some quiet place where we can be alone."

"Would you? I thought I'd like to introduce you to my friends."

Their long argument abruptly subsided with these last words. Kazu was moved. The pure and unadulterated sentiments of such a man stirred an almost ostentatious joy within her. "Very well," she said, "we'll do as you say. But how would it be if after the trip I invited everybody to the Setugoan by way of thanks for having been allowed to go along?"

"That's a good idea," Noguchi agreed without visible enthusiasm.

The party assembled at Tokyo Station on the morning of the twelfth before boarding the express train which was to depart at nine. Kazu was surprised to notice how young Noguchi looked. This was perhaps natural, considering that three of the five men present were over seventy.

Kazu had taken great pains with her clothes for the journey, which would mark, as it were, the first public announcement of her relations with Noguchi. She had the idea of dyeing some element of the name Yuken Noguchi into the design of her kimono. The only character of his name which lent itself to pictorial representation was *No*, or "meadow."

Kazu had begun her preparations well before the departure. After much thought she had decided that even if nobody else caught onto the meaning of a pattern connected with Noguchi's name, it would be sufficient if she alone understood. She ordered a kimono dyed with a pattern of white horsetails and dandelions on a black slubbed crepe, the plants shaded with gold paint, to suggest a spring "meadow." She wore a sash of light green striped silk, easy to fold and suitable therefore for a journey, and a sash clasp with a cloud ring pattern. Her plain gray cloak, patterned in narrowing vertical stripes, had a lining of grape purple. Her greatest ingenuity was devoted to the lining.

The white-haired octogenarian, a distinguished figure who deserved his reputation as the trail blazer among Japanese journalists, was treated with the utmost deference by the others. He was a Doctor of Laws, and moreover had published numerous translations of English literature. A cynic in the English manner, this old bachelor favored every form of social reform except for the anti-prostitution laws. He was one of the rare people who called Noguchi by a diminutive. The retired industrialist was an eccentric haiku poet by avocation, and the financial critic could be counted on for an unending flow of malicious gossip.

The old gentlemen were all congenial, neither ignoring Kazu nor making any obvious attempts to ingratiate themselves. The journey to Nara passed agreeably. The financial expert successively characterized different figures of the world of politics and finance as fools, blockheads, scoundrels, opportunists, mental incompetents, lunatics, wolves in sheep's clothing, smart alecks, misers without equals in history, cases of hardened arteries, simpletons, and epileptics. The conversation then turned to haiku.

"I can only look at haiku as a Westerner might," said the aged journalist. After a moment's pause for effect he continued, drawing on his encyclopedic memory, "There's a story in the *Chats on Haiku* by Torahiko Terada about a young German physicist who came to Japan on a holiday and fell in love with everything Japanese. One day he proudly announced to his Japanese friends 'I've composed a haiku,' and showed it to them. This is what he wrote:

> *In Kamakura*
> *Everywhere I went I saw*
> *Lots and lots of cranes.*

"To be sure, his haiku had the regulation five, seven, and five syllables, but it wasn't precisely poetic. My haikus are not a whole lot different from his. Here's one I thought up while listening just now to our friend here.

> *Our politicians*
> *And financial tycoons too—*
> *Fools the lot of them.*"

Everybody laughed, though if the same joke had come from the mouth of a young man nobody would have cracked a smile. When the conversation got onto the subject of haiku, Kazu became uneasy about the design on the lining of her cloak. She kept the cloak on, even though the railway carriage was warmly heated, for fear the lining might be seen. Before long the conversation drifted from the subject of haiku.

The men in their conversation laid an entirely excessive

emphasis on accuracy and minuteness of memory. Their conversation somehow reminded Kazu, listening without saying a word, of young men trying to outdo one another in boasting of their knowledge of women. These old men were at great pains to impart credibility to their remarks by insisting on a quite unnecessary precision, and by referring to meaningless details. For example, where a younger man would have been satisfied with a, "Let me see, it happened in 1936 or 37," these old gentlemen would relentlessly pursue the date. "Let me see, it happened in 1937, the seventh of June. Yes, I'm sure it was the seventh. A Saturday, I believe. I can remember getting off early from work."

The livelier the conversation became the more desperately they were obliged to struggle with natural decline, and these efforts on the surface at least resembled vigor. But in this respect too Noguchi was an exception. Kazu did not understand what could possibly interest him so in these men that he could enjoy their company; he alone maintained his youth by his dignity. As usual, he contributed an absolute minimum to the conversation, and if he became bored with a subject he would carefully count the segments in a tangerine he had peeled, and silently share the fruit with Kazu, giving her precisely half the segments. Even though Noguchi apportioned her the same number of segments, their size varied, and Kazu's share was actually less than half the tangerine. Kazu, suppressing her amusement, stared at the wrinkled bits of thin peel, the color of the harvest moon, still sticking to the fleshy fruit.

As soon as the train arrived in Osaka at half-past six that evening, the party boarded a car sent to meet them, and drove directly to the Nara Hotel. They had no time to rest before they all went to the dining room. Nara was unusually warm for this time of the year. Kazu had long since been schooled on the bitterness of the cold at the Omizutori ceremony, and was therefore no less delighted than the old men at the warmth of this evening.

The rites at the Nigatsu Hall begin each year on the

first of March, but they do not reach their climax until the night of the twelfth with the burning of the crate-like torches, followed by the dipping of the sacred water and the secret Tartar rituals performed early on the morning of the thirteenth. The ceremonies on the night of the twelfth attract the largest crowds.

The party hurried after dinner to the Nigatsu Hall, and was surprised to see how many people had already gathered below the hall. The crowd seemed less like participants in a religious ceremony than spectators at an extraordinary event.

The moment for the lighting of the huge pine-torches was at hand, and the party, guided by a priest, made its way in the darkness through the milling crowd under the platform of the Nigatsu Hall. Noguchi, taking Kazu's hand, marched ahead, oblivious of the precarious footing underneath. He bore no resemblance to the Noguchi who had hesitated to cross the road at Ueno; he feared cars but apparently not human beings. His bearing as he pushed through the rustic-looking people revealed his ingrained authority.

The distinguished guests were guided directly up to the bamboo grill erected to prevent the crowd from surging into the temple. Directly before them, just over the railing, a flight of stone steps led up to the platform where the ceremony would take place. The aged journalist, exhausted by the walk, clung to the railing to catch his breath. The newspaper executive, constantly worried about his old friend, had provided a small folding chair for him.

The climb had ruined Kazu's zori. The party stood now on sloping ground sparsely covered with dead grass, a sea of thawed mud, and Kazu, in order to protect her footing a little, clung to the railing. She turned her head and threw a smile at Noguchi, but his face was enveloped in the darkness. High above his head loomed the majestic balustrade of the platform and the swelling curves of the projecting eaves. The under parts of the eaves were mysteriously luminous. Clusters of stars were shining between the towering cedars around the hall.

Now the "Sevenfold Messages" were beginning. The chief votary, holding aloft a blazing brand, ran up and down the stone steps again and again, a bold figure in his girded-up robes. The stentorian voice proclaiming each of the "messages"—the offering of incense, the business of the ritual, the attendance at the worship, and the rest—combined with the dripping of the flames from the torches to complete the aura of solemnity. To these spectators who knew nothing of the ancient traditions of esoteric Buddhism or Dual Shinto, the somehow significant presence of the chief votary, his distracted bearing, his intent movements, all seemed like portents of a great calamity about to begin. Then, when the votary was gone and the torchlight no longer illuminated the stone steps, the utter desolation suggested that something would surely occur at any moment on the emptiness of the steps. Kazu was not especially devout and was seldom moved by anything she could not see with her own eyes, but as she stood there, clutching the bamboo railing, and looked up the stairs rising chilly and faintly white in the darkness, her eyes following them to the temple and platform above, she felt as if soon her heart would also mount the stone steps and share in some momentous happening in an invisible world.

Kazu, for all her good cheer and optimism, from time to time worried about what would happen to her after she died. She invariably linked such thoughts directly to her sins. Now, as she felt the warmth of Noguchi's overcoat pressing on her back and side, all the past love affairs which she had never before remembered in Noguchi's presence returned to life. Men had killed themselves for Kazu when she was younger. Some had lost their wealth and position, and others had sunk to the lowest depths of society, all because of her. Strangely enough, Kazu had never known love for her to ennoble a man or help him to success. Through no evil design on Kazu's part, men generally went down in the world once they met her.

Kazu's eyes were still on the stone staircase rising into the darkness as her thoughts turned to death. The past piece by piece crumbled away under her feet, and she was left with nothing to support her. If she went on in this way, there would probably not be a single person to mourn her when she died. Reflections on death convinced her that she must find someone she could depend on, have a family, lead a normal life. But the only way to do this was to go through with the formalities of love. She could not help tremble at the thought of still further sins. Only very recently—last autumn, it was—she had in the course of her promenade each morning at the Setsugoan looked at the world and at people with the same clarity as she surveyed the garden. She was absolutely convinced that nothing could disturb her anymore. But now she wondered if that transparency itself were not a portent of hell . . . The priest with them had explained that the Omizutori ceremony was from beginning to end a disciplinary rite of penitence and atonement. Kazu felt a personal awareness of what this meant.

The murmur arose around her that the torches were about to move out. The twelve immense torches had already been prepared and arranged beside the temple bathhouse. Each consisted of a huge bamboo, roots and all, some as big as a foot or more in circumference and twenty-five feet long. To the end of the bamboo trunk was fixed the torch itself, a circular crate over four feet in diameter.

Several priests in gold brocade capes with high triangular collars stood on the other side of the bamboo grill blocking Kazu's view. She tried to catch a glimpse between their shoulders of the arrival of the torches, but being by no means tall was unsuccessful. She whispered to Noguchi, "Lift me on your back, won't you?" Noguchi, smiling ambiguously, shook his head buried in his muffler. At that moment a roar went up and Noguchi's face was suddenly caught in the glare of flames.

Kazu hurriedly turned to see what had happened. The noise was caused by the ignition of the flames which now brilliantly illuminated the white walls of the temple, even to the cracks and scribblings, giving them a yellowish glow. A great sheet of flames suddenly blazed up before them, and the high-collared priests, shielding their faces from the fire with raised fans, turned into silhouettes. Exploding clusters of fire and the green cypress leaves atop the torches caught her eyes. The powerful arms of the youths bearing the enormous bamboo stakes glowed in the firelight. Kazu held her breath as she watched the mass of flames mount the stone steps.

The youths climbed the stairs, carrying on one shoulder the burning brands, which weighed close to 150 pounds. Cascades of sparks showered down, leaving crimson lotuses blossoming here and there on the steps. Sometimes the flames ignited a pillar of the roofed stairway and set it smoldering, only for a white-clad attendant following the youths up the steps to swab the flames with a broom soaked in water and extinguish the fire.

Kazu's eyes grew moist with excitement at the wild solitary beauty of the fire caught in the intent stares of the crowd swarming under the hall. With an inarticulate throaty moan she gripped Noguchi's hand in her sweaty hand. "Have you ever seen anything like it?" the words finally came out. "It was worth coming to Nara just for that."

Even as she spoke the bearers of the great torches, having reached the top of the stairs, paused a moment, leaning against the balustrade to the left of the passageway around the platform. Another roar of flames startled Kazu: a second phalanx of torchbearers had arrived at the foot of the stairs. In the meanwhile the youths on the platform had started racing frenziedly about like lions in flames, and with each shake of their brands showers of sparks descended on the heads of the crowd below. The fire leapt out toward the balustrade to the right, throwing a scarlet glow over the heavy overhanging eaves. The torches to the right for a moment seemed to burn somewhat less fiercely, only to be brandished into roaring flames again; the deep green of the cedars, caught in the swirl of flying sparks, acquired new intensity.

The crowd now emerged from the darkness in which it had been immersed, and loud-voiced invocations of the name of Buddha mingled in the general tumult. Sparks rained down like gold dust on the heads of the spectators, and the somber architectural grandeur of the Nigatsu Hall loomed over them.

"Isn't it wonderful?" Kazu kept repeating. Noguchi noticed that she was weeping.

It was close to daybreak when they returned to the hotel. They were too tired to wait for the early morning Tartar rituals which follow the Omizutori ceremony. Once back inside their hotel rooms they heard distant cockcrows, but dawn had not yet begun to whiten the sky.

Noguchi suggested that they bathe and then go to bed. Kazu, her eyes still shining with excitement, answered that she couldn't possibly sleep. She removed her cloak, started to fold it, then drew Noguchi's attention to the lining. Noguchi went up to the cloak spread out on the bed under the bright ceiling lamps. The grape-colored lining had a quiet beauty. Inscribed on it in white was a *hokku* written in a fairly skillful hand.

Noguchi asked, untying his necktie, "What is it?"

"It's a *hokku* by Sōgi. I had an artist write it especially for this trip. Spring's already here, you know." Kazu did not mention that the silk merchant had first suggested she use Sōgi's poem.

"*As long as you know,*" Noguchi read,

> "*As long as you know*
> *I am waiting, take your time,*
> *Flowers of the spring.*"

Noguchi stopped untying his necktie, and for a long while stared in silence at the poem. Kazu thought that his old dried-up hand with its prominent veins was beautiful.

"I see," he finally said. This was his only comment. That morning at dawn a man over sixty and a fifty-year-old woman slept in the same bed.

CHAPTER VIII

THE WEDDING

A week after her return Kazu, unable to restrain her impatience to make a return present, invited her companions of the journey to dinner at the Setsugoan. The menu served that evening was as follows.

HORS D'OEUVRES
Horsetail and sesame salad. Smoked carp
Butterball-flower rolls   Conger eel boiled in salt water
Perch on rice wrapped in bamboo leaves
SOUP
Clear soup with grated plums, star-shaped wheat gluten, chives, leaf buds
RAW FISH
Sea bream with skin, to suggest pine bark
Striped bass
BROILED DISH
Large prawns boiled in salt with raw mushrooms and peppers pickled in miso
BOILED DISH
Wakame *seaweed from Naruto cooked with new bamboo shoots and leaf buds*

She chose a particularly large room for the occasion, though there would only be a few guests. This, she knew, would be an evening to be remembered for many years, and she intended to give it a suitable setting.

Noguchi and Kazu had remained two more nights in Nara after their companions returned to Tokyo. They toured the various famous temples. One lovely morning they again visited the Nigatsu Hall and climbed the stone steps to the platform. The Omizutori ceremonies were virtually at an end now, and the youths who had performed so stirringly on the night of the festival, looking once again their usual selves—unsophisticated village boys—were sitting on the steps enjoying the sun. Seen from the platform, the slope below with its withered grass looked exactly like a field after a fire. Here and there patches of young sprouts spread blots of green ink, and next to them, partly burnt grass roots bathed in sunlight, displaying healthy blades.

Few words were exchanged during the walk. Noguchi's tone was quite unemotional, but the conversation, after shifting back and forth a while, resolved itself to a discussion of their marriage. Kazu did not let her emotions carry her away, but first listened carefully to Noguchi's opinion, then straightforwardly expressed her own. She had no intention, no matter what happened, of giving up the Setsugoan. On the other hand, a man of Yuken Noguchi's stature could not be expected to take up residence in a restaurant. Their married life would therefore have to be somewhat irregular. Kazu would go to Noguchi's house every weekend, and the couple would spend two days together. On Monday mornings Kazu would return to her place of work in Koishikawa . . . Such was the fair compromise they reached.

Thanks to the clear spring air and the calm of the ancient capital, the plans they worked out, the decisions they reached in their unhurried walks, were entirely reasonable. Kazu was astonished that such unexpected good fortune brought only a quiet happiness and no harsh agitation.

Kazu was about to become the wife of a distinguished man. She realized now that this was the long-dreamt-of goal of a lifetime. She was born in the country, in Niigata, and after losing her parents was taken in by a relative, a restaurant owner, as his adopted daughter. She ran off to Tokyo with the first man she had . . . After many years and hardships of every kind, Kazu had attained her present position; she was convinced now that she could eventually succeed in anything, once she put her mind to it. This conviction was clearly illogical, but in one way or another it had governed her life.

Until last autumn she had supposed that all of her hopes were already fulfilled, that her guiding conviction had outlived its usefulness. She had been surprised, however, to discover how unpredictably her heart had caught fire on meeting Noguchi, and she realized that one use still remained for her conviction.

Later on, Kazu was often to be looked at with suspicion and misunderstanding by society, precisely because of the strange coincidence between her affections and her great conviction. But it would be unfair to say that Kazu's love for Noguchi was utilitarian in nature or that her sole interest was in acquiring a distinguished name. Her love affair with Noguchi had in fact progressed so naturally that Kazu, acting as her inclinations led her and making no special effort to realize her dream, found that the dream had accomplished itself. She had hardly known what she was doing while she brewed the liquor, but when it was finally ready and she sampled it, she found it entirely to her taste. That was the whole story.

The misunderstanding arose from the excessively innocent joy which the excessively honest Kazu displayed over her marriage to Noguchi. She should have accepted it a little more sadly.

The night of March twenty-second was warm for the time of year. Noguchi came early and helped Kazu prepare for receiving the other guests. Even on such an occasion Noguchi was utterly self-composed. He sat in the dining room, Kazu beside him, and gave instructions, his face devoid of emotion.

Kazu said as she showed Noguchi the menu, "Today there'll be a special dish not on the menu. It's connected with the Omizutori. Unfortunately, it's rather heavy and if I serve it too late in the meal the guests won't be able to eat it. I'd be sorry to have that happen. On the other hand, I suppose you'd prefer to make the announcement toward the end."

"What connection is there between what I have to announce and this special dish?" Noguchi asked, a suspicious note in his voice. He was idly manipulating the fire tongs to poke a hole in the beautifully raked hibachi ashes.

"Don't you see?" asked Kazu, stammering, afraid as always of Noguchi's reaction. "If you make your announcement when this special dish has put everybody in a good mood, I think it'll really be stylish and produce a wonderful effect."

"Are you asking me to play a part?"

"No, nothing like that. It's just that I've thought of an unusual effect. They try for unusual effects even at tea ceremonies, don't they?"

"There's no need to play to the gallery. Can't you see that? I intend to make the announcement only to my most trusted and congenial friends. You should have told me from the start if you're trying for some fancy effect."

Kazu realized that her opportunity was slipping away. "Very well. I'll do as you say. In consideration for the guests' appetites I'll serve the dish immediately before the soup."

At that moment a maid announced the arrival of the newspaper executive and the octogenarian reporter.

Kazu welcomed these esteemed guests with a surprisingly radiant smile. The artistry with which she executed this instantaneous change from her pensive expression of a moment before and gaily sallied forth to meet the guests stunned Noguchi, but Kazu was too busy to notice.

The old journalist, as always, carried a leather satchel in his hand. His beautiful white hair fell over his ears, and he looked an impressive sight as he strode, perfectly erect, into the dining room, attired in formal Japanese clothes. The newspaper executive acted as if he felt that when in the old man's presence his only excuse for living was to play the part of the devoted retainer.

"Hello there, Noguchi," said the journalist. "That was quite a pleasant trip we took, wasn't it?" He went unhesitantly to the place of honor and seated himself. It was inconceivable that anyone else would sit there. Hardly had he settled himself than the conversation leapt far from the trip to Nara. The subject turned to the lecture delivered yesterday by the old gentleman at the special request of the Emperor on "The History of Japanese Newspapers."

"I couldn't go into exhaustive details in such a short time," the octogenarian commented. "As it turned out, the Emperor seemed most interested in the part on the Meiji period. It's sad to think of it, but the Meiji period seems to be the *gute alte Zeit* not only for us old folks but for the Emperor too."

"That's probably because it sounded like *die gute alte Zeit* from the way you talked," the newspaper executive volunteered.

"Perhaps so, but it's not very encouraging when the ruler of our country prefers any time to the present."

The other guests arrived in the midst of the discussion. Saké presently appeared, and the hors d'oeuvres were served. Kazu left the room briefly, and when she returned a few minutes later she was accompanied by two maids bearing a huge tray covered with blue flames. She proclaimed to the astonished guests, "Behold the torches of the Nigatsu Hall!"

The dish was a culinary triumph, intended above all to appeal to the eye. The torches, one for each guest, consisted of chicken meat to represent the bamboo poles, and broiled thrushes soaked in strong liqueur and ignited to form the burning crates on top. Fern shoots and other mountain vegetables were suitably disposed to represent the mountains around Nara. Even the little notice board enjoining riders to dismount before entering the Nigatsu Hall was in place.

The guests all praised Kazu's ingenuity. The industrialist, remarking that this year he had been able to witness the Omizutori ceremony twice, immediately composed an impromptu haiku on the subject. Kazu stole a glance at Noguchi's face.

Nothing could be more remote from joy than Noguchi's

expression at that moment. His face was agonized with choked emotions. The look he gave Kazu in response to hers was akin to hatred. But Kazu tranquilly withstood his glare, filled as she was with a rather brazen happiness. She knew that Noguchi's hatred had to do with a small point of honor—not allowing a woman to have her way.

Kazu suddenly stood and excused herself. She pretended she was going to the far end of the corridor, but in fact she hid herself in the next room, just the other side of the sliding doors. A moment or two later she heard Noguchi's voice. He said precisely what she had been hoping for. "I have a word for those of you here this evening. The fact of the matter is, I have decided to marry the proprietress of this establishment, Kazu Fukuzawa."

The momentary silence of the guests was broken by the laughter of the octogenarian bachelor. "I thought that Noguchi at least showed my genius for living, but I over-estimated him. Congratulations on not being a genius! Let's drink a toast. Where's the lady?" The old man shouted the words. Then, turning to the newspaper executive, he said reprovingly, "What are you waiting for? Telephone the office at once. It's a scoop for our paper, isn't it?"

"You still treat me as a cub reporter, after all these years!" protested the executive, at which everyone laughed. A mellowness had quickly spread over the gathering.

"Where's our hostess?" the old man shouted. Kazu had not heard such shouting from him during the journey, but she could guess from his voice that he was deliberately affecting the coarse, madcap manners of the turn-of-the-century student. Kazu thought that the time had at last come for her to return to the dining room. She bumped into the executive, hurrying off to telephone his newspaper. The mild-mannered executive as he passed Kazu gave her well-rounded shoulder a pinch, then ran on.

The news appeared in the next morning's newspaper. Genki Nagayama telephoned at once. "Good morning!"

he greeted her cheerfully, "How've you been keeping yourself these days? I happened to notice that article in this morning's newspaper. Not true, is it?"

Kazu remained silent at her end of the telephone.

"I see . . . I have something to discuss with you in that connection. How about coming to my office straight away?"

Kazu pleaded that she was busy, but such excuses had no effect on Nagayama. "I'm the one who's busy, and if I can find time to meet you, for your sake, it's your business to come here. I'm at my office in the Round Building."

Nagayama had what he styled offices in various places, by which he meant the reception rooms of his friends' offices. Surprisingly enough, no matter which "office" it happened to be, he merely had to press a bell to attend to many kinds of business, exactly as if he were the president of the firm, and Nagayama was equally demanding of the employees. Kazu knew the office in the Round Building, having visited it several times previously. It was the reception room of a large industrial fishing concern. The president came from the same part of the country as Nagayama.

The day was rainy and rather chilly, normal early spring weather. As Kazu walked through the peculiarly dismal row of shops on the ground floor of the Round Building, she noticed how the hallway, wet with rain-drops dripped from umbrellas, glimmered forlornly. There was something unfriendly and gloomy about the people passing by in their raincoats. The happiness Kazu felt this morning when she read the newspaper, so intense that she had actually made an offering to the household shrine, had been obscured without warning by this man she had supplied with money. Hadn't she given him whatever he asked for, without expecting anything in return? It was unfair, she felt.

Kazu felt depressed as she was riding up in the elevator, but when she actually confronted Nagayama's derisive smile, all tension disappeared and she became her radiant self. Kazu was glad now for this moment of the morning when she met, on a purely personal matter, a famous, extremely busy politician.

Nagayama unceremoniously blurted out, "There's no rhyme or reason in what you're doing. When did you decide to seduce this man without first getting your father's consent?"

"Oh—I thought you were my big brother, not my father. Well, father or brother, it's all one—you're a pretty conspicuous target and you're in no position to be lecturing me. I tell you that in advance."

It wasn't like Kazu to answer back, and her tone, a bit sharp, sounded unnecessarily brash. A smile never left Nagayama's fleshy face, which looked rather as if broken gobs of clay had been haphazardly affixed to it. By force of habit he painstakingly rolled and unraveled a cigarette as he spoke. "I can't imagine that at this stage you can be in such a hurry. After all, you're past the marriageable age."

"Yes. That's right—dozens of years past it."

After this exchange of pleasantries Kazu rather expected that Nagayama would next ask in the accents of the old-fashioned melodrama, "Are you really in love with him?" Then she would happily respond, "I am." Nagayama, convinced of everything by her answer, would not say another word . . . But Nagayama showed no signs of playing his cards that way.

Nagayama perpetually fidgeted. He was the one man whose cigarette Kazu never knew when to light. She always had a matchbox or matches ready in her hand, and no sooner did a man stick a cigarette between his lips than a flame that seemed to have ignited itself would at once be brought to his cigarette. But with Nagayama it was different; Kazu never managed to attune to his actions. His stubby fingers with their spatulate nails were forever playing with something. Sometimes it was a cigarette, sometimes a pencil, or it might be a document or a newspaper. At such times his eyes had the uncertain innocence of a baby, and his thick, brownish lips were turned down in a pout. Just when it appeared that he was at last about to put into his mouth the cigarette he had twisted and bent out of shape, it would be returned again to its original place.

Behind Nagayama's chair was a broad window opening on a panorama of rain-swept buildings. The heavy curtains of dark-green damask were pulled to either side. Bands of fluorescent lamps, lit since morning in the windows of the building across the way, shone through the rain, strangely close and bare.

"Supposing you marry Yuken Noguchi, what do you intend to do about the restaurant?"

"I'll go on running it as usual."

"You can't do that. Sooner or later there's bound to be a clash between the restaurant and Noguchi. The Setsugoan has kept going up to now mainly because of Conservative Party patronage, mine in particular. Don't you think it would be funny if the proprietress was the wife of an adviser to the Radical Party?"

"I've thought all about that. Why shouldn't I personally continue to be helped by the Conservative Party even if my husband belongs to the Radical Party? I'm told it's quite permissible under the new constitution for a husband and wife to vote for different parties."

"That's not the point. Don't you see that I'm worrying about your future? Anybody can see that you've drawn a blank. This marriage won't do either you or Noguchi any good. With your talents there's nothing you can't do, but instead you choose to shut off your whole future. Look, Kazu, getting married is like buying stocks. It's normal to buy when they're low—why should you want to buy stocks with no prospects for improvement? Noguchi in the old days was really impressive, no doubt about it. But today—to make an impartial appraisal—the proprietress of the Setsugoan is worth a lot more than the former cabinet minister, Yuken Noguchi. You should have some idea of your own worth . . . The one thing still like you is your decision to keep the Setsugoan going. You're not the type to shut yourself up in a house and act the dutiful wife. It's not written in your face."

"I'm well aware of that."

"I thought you would be. That much you can tell by looking in the mirror every morning . . . I wonder what Noguchi has in mind. I don't suppose he intends to take advantage of you."

The color mounted to Kazu's face. "There's nothing underhanded about him," she loudly retorted. "Don't judge others by your own standards."

Nagayama roared with laughter, not in the least annoyed. "Touché! But you've got to admit that I'm good at it. I get what I want without resorting to love-making."

Nagayama at last stuck the cigarette in his mouth. Kazu lit it. He took a puff, then, abruptly changing the subject, started on a pointless dirty story.

Nagayama's secretary came in to announce that the next visitor was waiting. Kazu picked up her shawl and stood up. Nagayama had in the end failed to say the words Kazu had been waiting for through the whole interview.

But Nagayama liked to give a warm, human note to his final curtains. Best of all, he enjoyed the illusion of capturing a human heart, and having coldly turned his eyes from Kazu to the rain outside, he looked back and called to her as she was going out the door, "Hey! You'll invite me to the wedding, I hope." He did not neglect his curtain line.

On the twenty-eighth of May Noguchi and Kazu were married.

CHAPTER IX

THE SO-CALLED "NEW LIFE"

Noguchi and Kazu were both equally unprepared for the wide publicity their marriage attracted. This was Kazu's first experience with the assaults of newspaper and magazine photographers, and Noguchi for his part was surprised that the world had still not forgotten him. On their honeymoon at the Gamagori Hotel they visited the Yaotomi Shrine on Benten Island. Kazu was about to make one of her usual extravagant donations when Noguchi firmly restrained her. He had reproved her, he said, because such behavior was vulgar. His brief reprimand had a frigid aristocratic tone which chilled Kazu's heart.

Their "irregular" wedded life began after their return to Tokyo. Every morning Kazu made a lengthy telephone call to Noguchi. Telephone calls failed, however, to diminish her innumerable sources of anxiety. Kazu, to reassure herself, consequently got rid of Noguchi's educated servant and replaced her with two maids and a houseboy, all three trusted employees at the Setsugoan. On occasion she would summon them to the Setsugoan and hear their reports on Noguchi's daily activities.

Every Saturday evening Kazu returned "home," bringing with her an immense stack of presents for Noguchi. It did not take long for the Noguchi household to be filled with unnecessary supplies of liquor and food. Kazu's periodic returns home were occasions for much commotion. She would make her entrance massaging her back and moaning about what an exhausting week she had spent and how hard it was to please customers. Then, throwing a glance around the musty, utterly unprepossessing room, she would declare, "Ah, there's no place like home, is there? I always breathe a sigh of relief as soon as I set foot inside the door."

It came as quite a shock to Kazu, however, when she learned that their Nara companions—though so generous with their felicitations once the old journalist had given the signal—were now spreading malicious gossip about her. They alleged among other things that during the trip Kazu had posed as Noguchi's wife without caring what the others might think, that she had shown respect only to Noguchi and slighted the others, that she had talked back rudely to the octogenarian, that the invitation to the Setsugoan itself, though ostensibly a "return present" was actually intended to advertise herself (there being no necessity to drag people off to the Setsugoan for a wedding announcement), that Noguchi was to be pitied ... Rumors of every kind reached her ears. When Kazu learned of this gossip she recalled the newspaper executive's pinching her after Noguchi made his announcement and felt as if the momentary sting—so funny and even pleasurable at the time—had now raised a purple welt on her shoulder. She passed her hand over the spot and angrily rubbed it.

She told Noguchi of the rumors. His reaction was to become furious. He declared that his only reason for having invited Kazu on the trip with the others and for having announced his marriage before them was that he trusted them all as friends. Kazu's transmission of such rumors was thus interpreted as a wife's attempts to divide her husband from his old friends. This was Kazu's first intimation that her husband's noble mind lacked sufficient powers of discernment.

An article ridiculing Noguchi appeared in a weekly gossip sheet. It claimed that Noguchi's abrupt switch to the Radical Party after the war had proved to be merely an unsuccessful publicity stunt, and his marriage to Kazu would prove another. Kazu was astonished that people could be so subtly malicious as to link the two events, but

Noguchi replied that it was best to ignore such attacks. He remained unruffled, at least on the surface.

Marriage had brought no fundamental change to Kazu's life. She kept on display in her room at the Setsugoan the photograph taken on their honeymoon and occasionally, during breaks between entertaining guests, would go to look at it. The picture showed the newlyweds standing on the stone steps at the southern end of Benten Island. They had brought a photographer along from the hotel to take the picture.

The photograph was barely a month old, but Kazu's appearance in the picture suggested that long-ago memories were posing for the benefit of future spectators. The memories already showed a certain coquetry. Kazu, noticing this, reacted against her all too restless nature, but the more she tried to suppress the intervening memories, the more vivid they became, and she finally let them have their way.

She and Noguchi had climbed beyond the Yaotomi Shrine, when suddenly the view, until then blocked by the trees, opened out before them in the clear early summer sunlight . . . Kazu, having just been scolded for her excessive donation to the shrine, was feeling quite dejected, and her relief was therefore all the greater at the sudden revelation of this brilliant landscape. "Ah, what lovely scenery! Just look. Isn't it wonderful?"

"We'll take the picture here," Noguchi immediately responded. The photographer, balancing himself precariously on the roots of a pine alongside the steps, readied his camera. Husband and wife, standing midway up the steps, gazed out at the sea. Before them lay the island of Oshima. The sea, encircling the Nishiura Peninsula to the west and Mount Kobo of Miya to the east, sparkled peacefully. The Atsumi and Chita peninsulas, wrapped in offshore haze, seemed to meet in the distance, making the sea look more like a lake than a part of the ocean. The numerous fish weirs jutting irregularly out of the water strengthened this impression. There were no clouds worth mentioning in the sky. The whole day seemed a moment carved unaltered and flawless from the eternity of Heaven, and set down before them.

The unbearably painstaking photographer kept them standing in the same position for an interminable length of time. Kazu noticed that Noguchi, who had been holding himself stiff as a statue all along, was conscious of the camera at every moment. After all the years of being chased by photographers he still kept this inborn rigidity. Kazu, by way of venting her anger at Noguchi's reprimand, took out her compact and rapidly inspected her face managing at the same time to edge the reflected glare from the mirror artfully from Noguchi's shoulder up to his strained cheeks. The tiny beam of light finally caught the corner of Noguchi's eye, and momentarily blinded, he relaxed his guard. At that instant the alert photographer snapped the shutter.

The picture now on Kazu's desk was not the one which caught Noguchi off-guard. Noguchi later obtained all the negatives from the photographer and discarded those he did not like. Kazu's photograph showed a perfectly staid middle-aged couple standing in early summer sea light. Kazu, somewhat stooped, was half hidden behind her husband's shoulder.

Kazu, surprisingly for a woman, was fundamentally unsure of the definition of happiness.

Her marriage involved no sacrifice, no confinement in a stranger's house, nor any annoyance from a mother-in-law or sisters-in-law, but married life had on the other hand not brought with it any surge of happiness. When she and Noguchi went out together as man and wife, she felt a joy she could not conceal. But when she attempted to track down the ultimate source of this social pleasure, she discovered that it was connected with the melancholy delight which stole over Kazu's heart in the middle of the wedding ceremony. Kazu kept her eyes lowered as she drank the ritual cups of saké to hold back the tears, but she was thinking all the while, "Now I'm sure to be buried in the grave of the Noguchi family! At last I've found some peace of mind!"

The magnificent garden of the Setsugoan faded from Kazu's thoughts, and its place was taken by the clearly perceived vision of a small, dignified gravestone. This explains Kazu's first request of Noguchi after their return from the honeymoon trip, a visit to the Noguchi family grave. Noguchi, who disliked going to the cemetery, put her off with various excuses but finally, one Sunday in the rainy season, Kazu managed to inveigle Noguchi into taking her to Aoyama Cemetery.

The day was gloomy with occasional showers of a powdery rain that gave the young leaves in the cemetery a fresh green look. Kazu and Noguchi, sharing one umbrella, followed the grave keeper along the path. He carried sprays of anise, incense sticks, and a pail of water for offering to the dead.

Kazu said, "I don't suppose the departed ones can sleep very peacefully what with all this endless flow of traffic right next to them."

"The family plot's fortunately in a slightly more secluded place," Noguchi answered.

The tomb, though not the imposing monument Kazu had envisioned, was of a gray stone carved with the family crest and showed something of the ancient lineage and pride of an illustrious family. Kazu was genuinely fond of such things. From stone to stone could be traced the genealogy, utterly untainted by fakery, of a splendid line of people. Kazu, protected by the umbrella Noguchi held over her, knelt before the tomb and prayed a quite unnaturally long time.

The smoke curling vigorously upward in the fine rain from the bundle of incense sticks caught in Kazu's hair and strayed among the locks. Its strong odor caused Kazu something like a vertigo of delight. What a truly immaculate, proud family! Kazu had had no opportunity even at the wedding to meet the living members of Noguchi's family, but she could imagine how the dead ones with their high principles and absolute incorruptibility had transmitted the family's heritage to succeeding generations. Grinding poverty, obsequiousness, lies, contemptible natures—these were no conern of this family. Confused memories returned of obscene parties in country restaurants, of drunken customers thrusting their hands inside an innocent girl's kimono, of a runaway girl shrinking in terror as she boarded a night train, of back alleys in the city, of bought caresses, of petty ruses of every sort employed to protect herself, of the domineering kisses of cold-hearted men, of contempt mixed with affection, of a persistent craving for revenge against an unknown adversary: such experiences were surely undreamed of by this family. No doubt someone in the family was eating in a French restaurant or feeding a pet canary even as Kazu, still a girl, was washing the underclothes of the woman she worked for.

Kazu now belonged to the same family as these people, and she would some day be buried in their family temple. And to think that she would dissolve into one stream with them, never to separate! What a source of comfort that was, and what a priceless trick on society! The comfort and the trickery would be completed when Kazu was actually buried there. For all Kazu's successes, her money, her prodigious largesse, people had never really been taken in by her. She had begun her career through trickery and in the end she would trick eternity itself. This would be the bouquet of roses Kazu would toss to the world . . .

At length Kazu unclasped her hands and rose from prayer. She examined the inscription on the side of the monument, and asked Noguchi about the most recent of the persons listed, "Sadako Noguchi. Died August 1946."

"It's my former wife. I'm sure you must've heard her name." Noguchi's expression was somber. He found it unnatural for Kazu deliberately to have asked such a question.

Kazu's next remark was even more unnatural. "That's right. Your wife is buried here too. I had forgotten." Kazu's voice was good cheer itself: it was precisely the high-pitched voice overflowing with energy that she used when giving orders to the maids at the Setsugoan. Not a trace of envy could be detected in this voice. Noguchi had to smile despite himself.

"Whom have you come to pay your respects to, anyway? You've never known any of these people."

"But they're your ancestors, aren't they?" answered Kazu with an unclouded smile.

On the way back from the cemetery they stopped in town and did some shopping. Kazu seemed in seventh heaven all that day, and was so playful that she startled Noguchi.

A deep languid sense of security began that day to creep over Kazu, and before long she had come gradually to neglect her work at the Setsugoan. Fortunately there were few guests, summer being the slack season. Suddenly she felt with terrible urgency that she was growing old.

The couple frequently took trips to the countryside to escape the heat, and wherever they went Kazu would exaggerate her emotions. By this exaggeration she suceeded only in isolating herself from Noguchi. It may be wondered if she was not mistaken in wanting to light a fire under the peaceful existence Noguchi craved.

Kazu had successfully seen to it that Noguchi was always kept in freshly laundered shirts, but her suggestions that the tailor make him some new suits were firmly rejected. Noguchi insisted that if suddenly after his marriage he were to appear in new clothes, people acquainted with the meagerness of his income would be quick to point at him with scorn. Kazu could not understand why it was wrong for her to use her money to order clothes for her husband. Noguchi was frequently obliged to caution her on that score. "You seem to think that giving people money will make them happy, but you're badly mistaken. Why can't you understand that the bigger the tip you give for some foolish reason, the more the other person will suspect your sincerity? The nature of my work is such that I must enjoy the full confidence of people, and this necessitates living simply. Please give up this snobbery of yours."

Kazu had the utmost respect for her husband's

character, but it was hard for her to see wherein lay the difference between his politics and those she had seen and heard at the Setsugoan. Her glimpses of Conservative Party politicians at the Setsugoan had inculcated in Kazu a splendid notion of the nature of their work. Politics meant pretending to step out to the men's room and then completely disappearing, forcing a man's back to the wall while cheerfully sharing the same fire, making a show of laughter when one is angry or flying into a rage when one is not in the least upset, sitting for a long time without saying a word, quietly flicking specks of dust off one's sleeve . . . in short, acting very much like a geisha. The exaggerated odor of secrecy clinging to politics confirmed its resemblance to the business of romance; politics and love affairs were in fact as alike as peas in a pod. Noguchi's brand of politics, however, was not quite romantic enough.

It was not in Kazu's nature, even though she neglected her work at the Setsugoan, to shut herself up in her house, to cook for her husband and patiently await his return. She often found herself wondering what to do with herself. She began to think that her customers connected with the Conservative Party were gradually drifting away. One of them in fact had said as much to her face. "I wish you'd persuade your husband to bolt the Radical Party and join us. We'd be glad to welcome back one of our senior statesmen, and we'd find it easier, for that matter, to come here. Don't you think you could move your husband if you put your mind to it?"

This was a very shabby way to speak of Noguchi, and Kazu bit her lip as she listened in silence. She thought, "It's my fault that a former cabinet minister should be treated like a restaurant owner." She brooded over the matter until finally she decided that wiping out the insult to Noguchi meant clearing her own honor. Then she turned to the valued customer and declared, "I have no desire to listen to such talk. Please be kind enough not to come here again."

Business setbacks owing to love or pride were, irrespective of magnitude, a new experience for Kazu. Her pride became more easily wounded each day. Kazu supposed that it was not merely her own pride that had become inflated, but that Noguchi's, added to hers, had doubled it.

One day late in autumn Kazu, spending her usual kind of weekend in Noguchi's house, suddenly jumped up and called him to the window. "Look, look—a crane's flying up there, a crane!"

Noguchi took no notice of her, but Kazu raised such a fuss that finally he reluctantly got up and looked out the window. He could see nothing. "Nonsense," he said, "do you suppose there'd be a crane flying in the middle of Tokyo?"

"I'm sure I saw one—a white crane with a red crest. It started to come down on the roof next door, but then it flew off again that way."

"You're out of your mind."

Thereupon the two began a rather gloomy argument. Kazu had missed her chance to admit playfully, "I was fooling you." She was as much to blame as Noguchi, and she had been mistaken to persist with such excessive earnestness and intensity in acting out her childish trick.

Kazu had finally realized at this late date how troublesome her disposition made things: she could not go on living unless she were constantly excited about something. The changes she tried to introduce into the routine of their lives were all rebuffed by her husband; Noguchi obstinately continued to lead his accustomed life. Even so, Kazu's affection for her husband remained unchanged. On Saturday evenings he sometimes showed a surprising loquacity, and though jokes were rare as ever in his conversation, he would on occasion discuss foreign literature or lecture her on socialism.

CHAPTER X

IMPORTANT VISITORS

It was obvious at any rate that Noguchi thought of this marriage as his final abode, and Kazu, for her part, felt she had found her tomb. But people cannot go on living inside a tomb.

During Kazu's normal weekdays at the Setsugoan the houseboy kept her informed in detail of Noguchi's activities. It came as a fresh surprise each time to discover how extremely uneventful his life was. Noguchi, despite his advanced years, devoted himself completely to his studies.

"Yesterday," the houseboy reported, "he spent from three in the afternoon until his bedtime in the library, studying. He ate his dinner in the library too."

"If he keeps studying that way I'm afraid he'll get sick from lack of exercise. I must give him a good talking-to next Saturday."

Kazu had strong prejudices concerning the intellectual life. For her it signified a kind of dangerous indolence into which men of promise were likely to fall. She rejoiced, however, that despite her intention of giving her husband "a good talking-to" he was not a man ever to listen to her advice.

About this time a little incident took place at the Setsugoan.

The night before there had been bright moonlight, and the thief had apparently concealed himself in the shadows of the garden to wait until everyone was asleep. The shrubbery around the huge ilex tree afforded an ideal hiding place. The thief had evidently sneaked into the garden when everybody was busy with the parties in full swing upstairs and the front entrance was left unattended. He must have spent a couple of hours quietly waiting. Probably he had refrained from smoking for fear that the lighted ends of his cigarettes might be seen, but Kazu discovered two or three wads of masticated chewing gum. From this she deduced that the thief was still young.

The thief had tried Kazu's room first, but after forcing open the window a couple of inches, he decided not to enter. Kazu's slumbers were undisturbed. There was a safe in her cupboard, but the thief could not have guessed that the occupant of such a cramped little room was the proprietress.

The thief then slipped into the sleeping quarters of the five resident maids. His shoe struck something soft, and the next instant powerful shrieks assailed him. He made his escape without stealing a thing.

Once the police arrived that night they created such an uproar that Kazu was unable to get back to bed again. It was during the course of her customary stroll the next morning that she discoverd at the base of the sunlit ilex tree, the lumps of chewing gum looking for all the world like glistening white teeth.

Kazu somehow couldn't get it out of her head that the thief, after looking into the room where she lay, had decided not to go in. To think that she had been sleeping all the while and knew nothing! In recollection, she was relieved, frightened, and also slightly dissatisfied. An empty suspicion rose within her as she felt the autumn wind pierce through her open sleeves to the base of her breasts, that the thief might have touched her body as she slept and then changed his mind. No, such a thing was unlikely. She was in the dark, and the window was open only two or three inches: there was no reason to think that he had gone so far as to examine her body.

But as she walked alone through the garden, the morning breeze playing on her, Kazu felt somehow the incipient decay of her flesh. She was exceptionally sensitive to the heat in summer, and had the habit of cooling herself by exposing directly to the electric fan not merely her breasts but her thighs, even before her maids or intimates. She could do this because she had confidence in her flesh. A shudder of doubt went through her now as she wondered about next summer. It seemed to her that marriage had made her body flabby.

It was at this point in her reveries that Kazu happened to look down and notice at the base of the tree some objects resembling human teeth. Kazu squatted down and discovered on careful examination that they were wads of chewing gum painstakingly rolled into balls. No guest or employee of the Setsugoan would chew gum in such a place, and the neighborhood children had no way of getting into the garden.

"They're the thief's," Kazu instantly guessed. The uncleanness of the gum struck her less vividly than the thought of the lonely hours the man had waited here. She even felt there was something very endearing about his loneliness. She could visualize the young, dissatisfied, strong, rough rows of teeth that had chewed the gum. The thief had chewed at time, at the dull rubbery society which did not admit him, and the uneasiness hanging over him. And there he waited in the lovely moonlight filtering through the leaves of the ilex tree.

Such unbridled fancy transformed the thief who had fled without stealing anything into Kazu's secret, unknown friend. The youth hidden in the moonlight, though terribly dirty, was a being whose wings had half sprouted.

"Why didn't he wake me, I wonder? If it was money he needed, I'd have given him all he wanted. If only he had said just a word to me!" Kazu felt somehow as if the young thief belonged to her circle of most intimate acquaintances. These were truly novel sentiments for Mrs. Yuken Noguchi.

Kazu started to call the gardener, then changed her mind. She decided not to tell anyone about the chewing gum—it might serve as evidence. She stripped some moss from the base of the tree and with her fingers carefully buried the wads of gum.

She waited until Noguchi's normal risng hour before making an unhurried call to report the incident. After describing briefly all that happened, Kazu added, "The police were certainly polite and considerate. I'm sure they'd never have bothered themselves that way over a thief breaking into a restaurant if it hadn't been for you." This was less Kazu's honest opinion than what she would have liked to believe. It was by no means clear whether the police were showing such courtesy to the proprietress of a restaurant patronized by the Conservative Party or to the wife of an adviser of the Radical Party.

Noguchi's comments as he listened to the report of the attempted burglary were extremely detached and superior. He spoke with the voice of an ambassador receiving word from a junior clerk of an automobile accident. "It's your own fault—you didn't make sure that the doors were properly locked," were his first words. Kazu, who had been hoping for some expression of relief that she was safe, was disappointed. Noguchi apparently considered sneak thieves and the like to be purely private household matters.

Such an attitude, as far as Noguchi was concerned, was fair and objective, but it struck Kazu as being extraordinarily cold. It aroused two kinds of reactions within her. The first was wounded pride to think that, after all the years she had run a restaurant by her unaided efforts, she should be criticized for not making sure that the doors were locked, of all things! The second was a fear that Noguchi had coldly seen through the strange emotional excitement she had been experiencing since the night before. But the next moment Kazu decided that the blame for her irritation lay with the telephone. Even at times when Noguchi was pleasant enough if you met him face-to-face, he would adopt a deliberately impersonal tone on the telephone.

"It's wrong when a married couple can only talk on the telephone," she thought. "Still, this kind of life was my idea in the first place."

Kazu listened distractedly to Noguchi's admonitions,

not intending to let them bother her. She examined her fingernails. There were, as always, clearly defined white crescents at the roots of her healthy nails, but she noticed today the cloudy, horizontal streaks on the nails of her middle and ring fingers." That's a sign I'll have lots of kimonos," she told herself.

Kazu all at once felt the meaninglessness of the large collection of kimonos she had already accumulated, a desolation as if her flesh were suddenly melting away.

The receiver still pressed to her ear, Kazu let her gaze wander. Morning sunlight streamed into the other rooms, and she could see the maids conscientiously dusting. The ridges of the new tatami were glossily defined in the early sunshine. At that moment a duster flickered over the openwork carving of the transom . . . The sunlight accentuated the smooth, persistent movements of the young maids, their backs stooping and rising in the rooms and corridors.

"Are you listening to me?" Noguchi demanded, his voice rather sharp.

"Yes."

"Something's come up here too. I've just had word that two important guests are coming tonight. You'll have to receive them."

"Will they be coming here?"

"No, to the house. I want you to order a dinner, return home and receive them."

"But . . ." Kazu enumerated the important customers who had reservations for the Setsugoan that evening, and started to explain why she couldn't possibly leave the restaurant.

"I think it's a good idea for you to return when I tell you to."

"Who are these important guests?"

"I can't tell you on the phone."

Kazu was exasperated by such secrecy. "Can't you? You can't tell your wife the names of your guests? Very well, if that's the way you feel."

Noguchi answered in a voice of unbearable frigidity, "You understand me? You're to have dinner ready and return home by five o'clock. I won't take no for an answer." With these words he hung up.

Kazu was so annoyed that she remained for a while sulking in her room, but eventually it occurred to her that this was the first time Noguchi had broken their agreement under which she returned home only for the weekends. The guests must certainly be very important.

Kazu reached out her hand and opened the window a couple of inches. This was the same window which the police had the previous night searched for fingerprints. Somebody—the thief or a policeman?—had trampled the small yellow chrysanthemums under the window. Some of the flowers were imbedded in the soft earth like inlaid work, quite unblemished, their shapes as clearly defined as those in a heraldic design. Here and there the yellow of a petal had straightened itself and risen from the ground.

An irresistible drowsiness came over Kazu, and she lay down on the tatami under the window. She turned her eyes clouded with anger and sleeplessness toward the bit of sky visible through the barely opened window. The morning sky radiated a distant and serene light. The cloudiness in Kazu's eyes traced ripples across the sky. She thought, "I don't need one more kimono. What I want now is something very different." So thinking, she fell asleep.

Kazu returned "home" after all. To mollify the customers expected that evening, she left word that she had gone home with a fever. She then directed the maids who would accompany her home to carry with them large quantities of the menu for the day packed in lacquer boxes.

Noguchi was in a surprisingly good humor when she arrived, and mentioned quite freely the details he had refused to divulge on the telephone. The guests were the Chief Secretary and Executive Director of the Radical Party. He could more or less guess the nature of their business with him, and he had decided, since he would have to refuse their request, to express his regrets by offering them hospitality at his home. The secret matter which Noguchi had refused to discuss on the telephone amounted, then, to nothing more than this. Such caution at once revealed to Kazu the delicacy of her husband's political position.

The guests knocked at the gate of the Noguchi house as it was growing dark. The faces of Kimura, the Chief Secretary, and Kurosawa, the Executive Director of the Radical Party, were familiar from political cartoons, and Kazu had already met them at the wedding. Kimura looked like a gentle, doddering old preacher, and Kurosawa resembled a coal miner.

Kazu, accustomed as she was to Conservative Party politicians, found it somehow unbearably funny that Radical Party politicians also exchanged the usual polite greetings when they met, and observed normal etiquette on entering a house. There was something false about these actions, as if they were calculated to throw people off their guard. Kazu found Kimura's smiling, soft-spoken behavior particularly puzzling. Something about his appearance and manner of speech recalled a quiet old tree dropping a leaf or two in the sunlight every time a gentle breeze stirred its branches.

The two guests showed Noguchi the deference due a senior. Kimura refused again and again to sit in the place of honor, and could only be persuaded with much difficulty.

Kazu sensed that a certain dryness of the skin was common to all three men, including Noguchi. Their skins were parched by long absence from positions of real authority, as some men's skins are parched by long absences from a woman's body. Their polite greetings and gentle smiles were darkened by the shadow of an enforced asceticism; Kimura's gestures of the old professor and Kurosawa's rather ostentatious simplicity were both rooted in the same life of asceticism.

Kimura politely praised the meal, a mark, Kazu thought, of his social ineptness. Noguchi displayed his usual nervous reaction, his face plainly revealing his embarrassment that cooking that was not his wife's should be praised. As for Kurosawa, he merely munched away in silence.

"I'm no tower of strength," Noguchi was saying. "You're badly deluded if you think I'd make a strong candidate. I'm the forgotten man."

Noguchi's tipsiness, increasing with each successive cup of saké, showed itself in the proud repetitions of such disclaimers, and each time Kimura and Kurosawa almost mechanically expressed simultaneous dejection.

Kazu poured the saké for the party, as Noguchi had commanded. It only gradually dawned on her that Noguchi's disavowal, repeated every five minutes, was being made for her benefit; she was aghast at her own obtuseness. She surely must have recognized ever since her first meeting with Noguchi his old-fashioned, obstinate bashfulness. He undoubtedly felt that to reveal to his wife in the presence of others his political ambitions was no different from letting others see his sexual desire.

Kazu immediately found some casual pretext to step out of the room. She returned to her own room, summoned a maid, gave orders. When the maid had departed, Kazu was left with nothing to do, and she began listlessly to tidy up. Kazu kept Noguchi's personal accessories in one of the drawers of her bureau. Three little boxes filled with his old, foreign-made cuff links were in the drawer.

Kazu, to pass the time, emptied out the different sets of cuff links on a small table. One set was in solid gold with the royal coat of arms of some small European country, another had precious stones, another in gold—apparently the gift of a Japanese princely family—was shaped like a chrysanthemum, and one set consisted of carved ivory images of Shiva . . . All were probably gifts, but they made up an odd collection.

It was like a collection of shells picked up on summer strands at many places, old remembrances of the sea. Noguchi's wrists, which they were to adorn, were withered and mottled now, but the shells would always harbor reflections of bygone sunsets. Kazu flicked them like marbles with her fingertips, and listened to the faint, cold clinks when they collided. She wondered if she couldn't play chess using the cuff links for pieces. Her first choice for the king was the cuff links with the unicorn crest of the small European kingdom. The imperial chrysanthemum cuff links would be the queen, she decided, but somehow this didn't seem right. The imperial chrysanthemum would have to be the king, after all . . .

"I'm sure he'll accept," Kazu thought, guided mainly by her political intuition. A joyous excitement welled up inside her. The heavy intellectual walls of Noguchi's study separating him from herself were surely about to crumble. And, just as surely, the day was coming which would demonstrate that their lives had not already come to a close.

"I'm sure he'll accept!" Kazu was instantly convinced. She could hear from the room across the hall the unfamiliar sound of Noguchi's laughter mingled with that of the guests. Kazu deliberately slid open her door and looked toward them. In the lamplight spilling into the hall from the sitting room, waves of rather mournful laughter, like fits of coughing, could still be heard.

The guests departed about an hour later. Kazu thoughtfully telephoned for a hired limousine to drive them back. Noguchi saw the guests to the door, Kazu accompanied them all the way to the front gate. The cold wind had intensified since nightfall, and beyond the clouds frantically scudding back and forth in the sky was the moon, like a drawing pin stuck into a wall.

Kimura's face under the dim gate lamp looked small and mouselike. The face as a whole was almost immobile, but around his mouth the flesh was curiously pliant and elastic, and when he muttered something in a low voice, this flesh with his mustache would hover unnecessarily around the words.

Kazu, catching him by the shoulder of his suit, abruptly pushed him against the wall. She whispered, "You'll trust me, won't you, even though I run a restaurant for the Conservative politicians?"

"Of course, Mrs. Noguchi."

"Has my husband agreed to run in the gubernatorial election?"

"You certainly know what's going on! I'm astonished. We couldn't get an immediate answer, but he promised to give us his decision in the next couple of days."

Kazu pressed her clasped hands to her breast girlishly. The gesture signified that she was tightening into a plan the thoughts which had flashed into her mind, as she might tighten a loose knot. "Please persuade my husband somehow. As far as money goes—excuse me for mentioning this—please leave everything to me. I promise I shan't cause the Radical Party any trouble."

Kimura started to say something, but Kazu had a gift of getting the jump on people in conversation and thereby effectively preventing them from interrupting. "But you mustn't say a word of this to my husband. Please keep it an absolute secret. I accept full responsibility on that one condition."

After delivering these remarks with lightning rapidity, Kazu suddenly raised her voice and, intoning the customary parting salutations in clear tones audible as far as the front door, she bundled the guests into the car. "Oh, dear," she cried, "doesn't the Radical Party provide you with someone to carry your brief case? Such a heavy brief case to hold on your lap! Well, I must say."

These final observations were in fact the only ones which reached Noguchi standing in the entrance, and Kazu was later reprimanded for these uncalled-for comments.

CHAPTER XI

"THE NEW LIFE"— THE REAL THING

A new feature was added to the daily routine of the Noguchi household. Every Monday a man named Soichi Yamazaki came to deliver a two-hour lecture mainly concerned with the administration of Tokyo Prefecture. Noguchi would open his notebook like a diligent junior high school student and, listening attentively, take painstaking notes, using a fountain pen he had bought twenty years before. All week long he studied intently, reviewed his lessons, and did absolutely nothing else.

Soichi Yamazaki was a protégé of Committee Chairman Kusakari, at whose suggestion he was dispatched to Noguchi's house. This master of campaign strategy was completely uninterested in working in the public eye; a disillusioned former Communist, he had developed into a daring, alert, red-faced practical politician who turned his back on theories of any kind. Ever since Yamazaki began his visits Kazu had made it her practice to take off Mondays—in other words, to prolong by one day her absence from the Setsugoan. Her first glance at Yamazaki's face told her that she had found in him the kind of man who could vow a lasting friendship with no romantic complications. He was dynamic, but with a human touch, rather reminiscent of Genki Nagayama. He was the first of this type Kazu encountered in the Radical Party.

Yamazaki's human touch was born of political despair. It was strange that it should accidentally resemble so closely the Conservative politicians' touch, born of an incurable optimism. Kazu instinctively recognized this indispensable attribute of the practical politician. She at once became friendly with Yamazaki.

A telephone call by Genki Nagayama to the Setsugoan had brought Kazu her first knowledge of her husband's decision to stand for office. Nagayama, laughing on the wire, plunged directly into the conversation. "What a crazy decision! Yes, your husband's really made a blunder, hasn't he?"

Kazu's instinct told her at once that he referred to Noguchi's candidacy in the election for governor, and it wounded her to think that even before her husband told her the news it had reached the ears of her old acquaintance, Noguchi's thick-skinned "political rival." Kazu pretended not to know what Nagayama meant, but deliberately played the part badly. She played it in such a way as virtually to proclaim, under the thin disguise of feigned ignorance, her joy and pride in her husband's decision. At the same time she adroitly and politically shifted the resentment she then felt toward her husband for his indifference. "What's all this about a blunder?" she demanded. "If my husband's been unfaithful, just let it pass. I'm shutting my eyes to such things, and I intend to keep them shut all the way."

Nagayama, taking no notice of her artifice, related the bare facts. His tone was not like the old Nagayama's, and seemed to reveal a change of attitude. "Anyway, he's made a foolish decision. It'll ruin him politically. What do you intend to do about it? Please, as his wife, urge him on bended knees to change his mind. All right? I'm telling you as an old friend."

With that he hung up.

During the following days Committee Chairman Kusakari called at the Noguchi house, and the Chief Secretary also paid several visits. The houseboy provided Kazu at the Setsugoan with a detailed register of all Noguchi's visitors, stating the time of each visitor's arrival and departure, indications of his business with Noguchi, and the master's humor at the time—everything.

Three days after Nagayama's telephone call, news of

Yuken Noguchi's candidacy appeared in the press. It was utterly typical of Noguchi, but that evening, after the news had already been publicly reported, he summoned Kazu home from the Setsugoan, and when the two were alone in the parlor, he informed her, as if he were revealing an immense secret, of his decision. He assumed as a matter of course that his wife never read the newspapers. Noguchi had absolutely no grounds for this belief, but it was normal for him to decide, for example, that Kazu disliked dogs when she did not, or to assume arbitrarily that she liked fermented soybeans, a dish she could not abide. Noguchi, a victim of illusions he himself had created, had apparently come to be convinced that his wife was uninterested in politics.

Kazu listened with the air of one hearing important news for the first time to his proclamation delivered in samurai accents, then made the brave reply—contrary to Nagayama's suggestion—"Now that you have accepted, I hope you will throw yourself into it completely."

Ever since the morning she had received Nagayama's telephone call, Kazu had become the captive of her daydreams. The flames of vitality were lit anew; the tedium of her moribund life had vanished without a trace, and she sensed that days of struggle with her own reckless impulses had begun.

It had been an unusually warm day for winter. Kazu went that afternoon to a piano recital given in Ginza Hall by the daughter of a certain industrialist, a patron of the Setsugoan. As Kazu looked down from the fifth-story window at the twilit Ginza, the unfamiliar rear view of its uneven line of roofs plainly visible, she felt for the street an affection it had never previously inspired in her.

Here and there neon lights had begun to glow, and at a construction site in the distance the steel framework and cranes reaching diagonally across the pale blue sky were dotted with twinkling little lights: the view before her looked exactly like some weird harbor floating over the land. A red and white balloon, which had been resting from its daytime labors on the roof of a nearby building, was now beginning an unsteady ascent into the evening sky, trailing a long pennant with a neon advertisement.

Kazu noticed many people moving about in the early evening light above ground level. Two women in identical red coats were climbing the emergency stairs at the rear of a building. A woman with a baby strapped to her back was taking in the shirts left on the line behind a billboard atop some business establishment. Three men in white chef's hats emerged onto a dirty roof and lit each other's cigarettes. Nobody was sitting on the chairs by the windows on the fourth floor of the new building across the way, but Kazu caught a glimpse of the feet of a girl wearing red socks as she crossed a green carpet in the back of an office. There was something curiously peaceful about the movements of all these people . . . Chimneys on the rooftops high and low sent up columns of smoke which rose perpendicularly into the almost windless sky.

"I'll burrow my way into the hearts of each and every one of them," Kazu thought, intoxicated by her dream fantasy. "Wouldn't it be wonderful if I could make each of them cast his ballot for Yuken Noguchi! If only I could grab them all in one swoop, right from here! I know that their heads are filled with their love affairs, or worries about money, or thoughts about what they'd like to eat tonight, or their movie dates . . . but somehow I must carve the name of Yuken Noguchi into one corner of their minds. I'll do anything for that. It doesn't bother me what people will think or what the law has to say. The distinguished gentlemen who patronize the Setsugoan have all succeeded without worrying about such things."

Kazu's breasts swelled under her stiff Nagoya obi, and her fantasies had given her eyelids a puffed, drunken look. She felt as if her feverish body were gradually spreading out in the darkness to engulf the great metropolis.

The bedroom of the Noguchi house had been furnished with twin beds since the wedding. The beds were installed on an old Persian rug, and when Kazu, who was accustomed to sleeping on the floor, lay on her back and looked up at the ceiling, it seemed strangely close, and the walls were strangely oppressive.

Noguchi invariably fell asleep first. Kazu would then switch on the lamp by her pillow, not to read a book or a magazine, but to induce sleep by staring fixedly at something. Sometimes, for example, she would stare at the catches of the sliding doors, shaped like half-moons and delicately worked in metal like swordguards. The catches had for their designs the "four gentlemanly flowers"—plum blossom, chrysanthemum, orchid, and bamboo. The one closest to her was the orchid; in the dimly lit room the blackened metal orchid confronted Kazu's sleepless eyes.

She had turned off the gas stove a while before, and its warmth now ebbed away like the receding tide. In the course of a similar night, quiet like all their weekends, Noguchi had finally decided to run for office—but by what process of reasoning, his wife had absolutely no way of guessing. His behavior before accepting the nomination, during his deliberations, and after acceptance showed a magnificent uniformity. Even Noguchi must surely have been nervous and worried, must have changed his mind only to revert to his former opinion, but to his wife he revealed nothing of this. All he let her see was his usual spell of coughing before retiring, his usual half-hearted caresses and opaque manner of approach, his usual resignation, his usual sleeping posture, curled up like a dormant chrysalis. Noguchi's bed suggested somehow a windswept station platform. All the same, he got to sleep more easily than Kazu.

Kazu's twin bed by comparison suggested a roaring fire. Her body was feverish, not so much with sexual desire as with unbridled imagination. She found it pleasantly cooling to stretch out her hand and touch the dark metal of the orchid. The delicate profile of the chasing transmitted in the dark to Kazu's fingertips a sensation of stroking a small, hard, expressionless, fastidious face.

"Yes," Kazu thought, "tomorrow is Monday. Tomorrow I'll get hold of Yamazaki and start my operations."

At three o'clock on Tuesday afternoon Kazu secretly met Yamazaki on the mezzanine of the Shiseido, a tearoom in the Ginza.

Yamazaki's description of the meeting may be found in *The Election in Retrospect*, the book he later published. "I had previously called a number of times at Noguchi's house, and was favorably impressed by his wife's lively, frank disposition. But the first time I met Mrs. Noguchi alone on the outside, I noticed as I climbed the stairs to the mezzanine of the Shiseido that despite her usual liveliness and energy, she seemed like a terribly lonely woman. It was extraordinary that at this moment, when her head was filled with plans for her husband's election campaign, she should have created such an impression of solitude. When we began to talk (we did not say a word that was not related to the election), she spoke with her habitual impassioned eloquence and overwhelmed me in a matter of moments."

Kazu had made a list of items to ask Yamazaki, and she fired her questions straight as arrows. There were probably six to ten months before the election, but this was up to the present governor, who might resign at any time. Kazu personally intended in the meanwhile, though she realized it was prohibited by law, to push forward a pre-election campaign, keeping this a secret from Noguchi. She had such-and-such an amount of money available for this purpose, and she was resolved, in case this should prove inadequate, to mortgage the Setsugoan forthwith. She wanted specific advice on the most effective pre-election campaign, one which would stay clear of the clutches of the law.

Yamazaki gave her systematic instructions. "First, have some visiting cards—especially big ones—printed with your husband's name in the largest available type."

"Depend on me for that. Would you mind stopping with me at the printer's on our way back?" Kazu spoke breathlessly.

"Would you like an idea of how big a proposition it is to elect a governor of Tokyo? Just supposing you stick two posters on each telegraph pole in Tokyo. There must be 150 or 160 thousand telegraph poles. That means you'll need 300,000 posters. Each poster costs three yen—that makes 900,000 yen—and figuring one yen apiece for the men who stick on the poster, it comes to a total of 1,200,000 yen. That alone is enough money to run a small election." Yamazaki was quick to cite figures apropos of anything, and they often convinced people.

Kazu's insistence on discussing in a loud voice the possibilities of a pre-election campaign and ways of evading the law, quite oblivious of the people at the next table, made Yamazaki look nervously around them. Aware of the danger, he proposed a return condition: in exchange for his promise to keep all Kazu's activities—her financial support and everything else—a secret from Noguchi, he requested that henceforth she consult with him beforehand on every step, however trifling. Kazu agreed.

"I feel better, now that we've had this frank talk," Kazu said, with a cheerful pat on her obi. "There's no getting around it, my husband simply doesn't understand the hearts of the ordinary Japanese people. He reads foreign languages and studies in his library, he's a born gentleman, but he doesn't understand the feelings of his own maids. Am I wrong in thinking that you and the others understand only with your heads? But it's no problem for me to slip straight into the hearts of the common people. Why, I've even peddled fried fish balls when I was down on my luck. How about it, Mr. Yamazaki, I don't suppose you've ever peddled fried fish balls, have you?"

Yamazaki, embarrassed, gave a sheepish grin. "Logical arguments can reach only a limited area. We need emotional weapons to capture the five million qualified voters, and you certainly have them, Mrs. Noguchi. You're a big comfort to all of us."

"You don't have to pay me any foolish compliments, Mr. Yamazaki," Kazu murmured sensuously, lifting her sleeve to her face in mock embarrassment. Then she continued with premature professional experience, "We can worry about party policies and the rest later on. The only important things in an election are money and feelings. I intend to attack with just those two weapons. I'm only an uneducated woman, after all, but I've got enough warmth in me to divide among five million people and still have some to spare."

"I understand you perfectly. I hope you'll plunge recklessly ahead."

Kazu was pleased to recognize in Yamazaki the mature man's half-baffled generosity toward a woman. "Make the maximum use of me, please. You'll find that I'm a woman worthwhile using." Kazu's tone seemed to terminate the discussion.

Yamazaki drank his coffee and ate a great wedge of strawberry shortcake to the last crumb. It reassured Kazu to see a ruddy-faced man, necktie firmly in place, eat a big piece of cake.

Kazu then suggested that he should know her personal history, and for about an hour she held forth, summarizing all her troubles since she was born. This frankness, as it turned out, amply justified itself, for it later induced Yamazaki to stand by her with more loyalty than he would have shown otherwise.

Kazu's frankness and honesty easily became exhibitionist before a man she did not especially love. She deliberately affected this mannerism in order to destroy any illusions people might have about her, but it was hardly likely that anyone would entertain illusions about Kazu. There was a plebeian warmth to her plump beauty: not having a single weak spot, it retained, regardless of the jewelry or splendid clothes with which it might be adorned, the fragrance of black loam, a heritage from her native soil. As a matter of fact, this impression of physical opulence saved her chatter from being annoying, and made it seem instead a complementary feature.

Yamazaki was a good listener. Kazu had the impression when talking to him that her words were not slipping through his face as through a sieve, but sinking deeply and certainly into the heavy face with its unchanging smile. Kazu said, "Please feel free to tell me anything with absolute frankness." During her short married life Kazu had already developed a hunger for frankness.

Noguchi suspected nothing. He could remain entirely ignorant because he made no effort to learn anything beyond what directly met his eyes and ears. His lordly indifference of the *grand seigneur* (or of the high-ranking bureaucrat) permitted Kazu to dispense with elaborate precautions to keep her activities secret from him. Five days of the week, moreover, she was away at the Setsugoan.

Kazu's heart, however, was less and less in the operation of the Setsugoan. She raced about incessantly in her car and met Yamazaki often. His slumbers were not infrequently disturbed late at night by a telephone call from Kazu, acting on sudden inspiration.

As for Noguchi, two hours of the week, as usual, he listened attentively to Yamazaki's lecture, and the rest of the time he did nothing. It had been decided that all questions of policy, campaign funds, and election personnel were to be handled through Yamazaki, who was therefore in a position to give Noguchi advice on every subject. Noguchi, truly imbued with a spirit of respect for the law, intended to refrain from any campaigning until the election was officially proclaimed. The secret meetings of the Kazu and Yamazaki were, however, well known to the leaders of the Radical Party. They issued instructions to Yamazaki, their policy being to let Kazu do what she pleased, providing she did not get out of hand. The Radical Party had never before had a powerful backer with so much money and enthusiasm and who, on top of everything else, was a woman. When word occasionally reached Noguchi's ears of activities resembling a pre-election campaign, he assumed that they were financed entirely by Radical Party funds. Having spent half of his life on money provided by the national budget, "public funds" to him suggested appropriations so enormous one could not possibly use them all up.

The visiting cards were ready in a day or two. Kazu distributed them to cigarette stands and to waitresses in restaurants. One day when Yamazaki was riding with Kazu in her car, she ordered the chauffeur to stop before a large, long-established bakery. She went in and Yamazaki followed. Kazu bought 3,000 yen worth of jelly rolls, too many to carry by herself. Yamazaki, picking up bags of jelly rolls in both hands, was astonished to see Kazu produce one of the extra-large visiting cards and offer it to the proprietress, saying, "This is my husband's card. I hope you won't forget us."

Once they were back in the car Yamazaki said, "That was certainly a surprise, Mrs. Noguchi. Don't you know that the owner of the bakery is a Conservative member of the prefectural assembly?"

"Is he? I had no idea. Well, I'm sure I've at least succeeded in confusing the enemy."

"What do you intend to do with all these jelly rolls?"

"I'm taking them to the Koto District Orphanage."

"Orphans can't vote, you know."

"But they have lots of sentimental adults around them."

Yamazaki accompanied Kazu without protest to the orphanage, where he was again obliged to witness a display of the extra-large cards.

Kazu came to be a familiar figure at festivals, beauty contests, and every other kind of public gathering in the prefecture. She even sang on request. She attended housewives' meetings dressed as a cook, and won her way into the hearts of these simple people too insensitive to detect the ruse.

Kazu showed herself extremely critical of the Radical Party's failure to win general support except among the intellectuals. When informed that the party was weak in Koto District and in the Santama rural districts, she felt convinced that here were corners where many hearts beat which only she, Kazu, could capture. She would frequently ask Yamazaki, "Haven't we any good contacts in Santama?"

One late spring day Yamazaki brought the following

intelligence. "I'm told that the cornerstone of a monument to the war dead has just been laid at Omé in Santama. They're going to hold a memorial folk song festival in the park, and the local folk-dance teacher, who's originally from your part of the country, says she'd like to invite you to attend."

"We couldn't wish for a better opportunity. I'll go in a kitchen apron."

"I wonder if a kitchen apron is quite the appropriate costume for a folk-song festival. I'll check on that."

Each activity of this kind Kazu participated in, each disbursement of her money, was based on cool calculation, and however spontaneous an expression of human kindness it might appear, her purpose was invariably the same; to use people in order to win the election. Such was Kazu's deliberate intent, but she did not reckon on the powerful impression which her self-sacrificing enthusiasm readily produced on people. She would laugh in her sleeve when she listened to people who had genuinely been moved, but when she discovered that some people were saying that she was devoid of honest feelings and governed entirely by calculated expedience, she was furious that her motives should be so misunderstood. This was one respect in which Kazu's psychology was surprisingly complicated.

One thing Kazu herself failed to anticipate was that her tactics, despite their simple hypocrisy, would prove the major reason that audiences loved her. What Kazu imagined to be her calculation proved to be a kind of sincerity, a sincerity with a peculiar attraction for the masses. Regardless of her motives, her devotion and fervor had the special property of ingratiating her with the people. As a matter of fact, Kazu had little confidence in her detachment. Her obvious stratagems, her reckless attempts to trick people, her shameless, persistent repetitions of her different artifices—these failings actually led simple people to relax their vigilance. The more she tried to exploit the common people, the more they loved her. People might talk behind her back where she went, but she left a mounting popularity. When Kazu decided to appear before the housewives of Koto District wearing an apron, she herself supposed that she was a lady deliberately dressing herself in an apron in order to hoodwink people and to mix the more readily with them. However, the people were not deceived: an apron suited Kazu very well!

One magnificently clear afternoon in late spring Kazu and Yamazaki took a two-hour drive to the city of Omé. While in the car Kazu, as usual, showed Yamazaki the packet wrapped in thick Japanese paper. "Do you suppose 100,000 yen would be the right amount to offer for the war monument?"

"Don't you think it's too much?"

"The monument's being put up by the families of the deceased, not only from Omé, but from the whole Santama area. It may be too little, but it's certainly not too much."

"It's your money. You're free to use it as you please."

"There you go again with your cold comments. My money, when you come down to it, is now the party's money."

Yamazaki always had to take off his hat to such devoted and loyal sentiments. All the same, of late a note of irreverent sarcasm had crept into his conversations with Kazu. "No doubt when you stand before the foundations of the war memorial a flood of tears will gush forth again, quite naturally."

"Of course. And naturally too. Nothing makes an impression on people unless it's natural."

As they neared Omé the patches of green along the road became more extensive, and they were particularly struck by the beautiful elms they could see here and there. The elms stretched delicate branches high into the blue, and the clustered twigs had the sharp clarity of countless cast nets simultaneously thrown into the sky.

Kazu, enjoying her first excursion into the countryside in a long time, kept pressing on Yamazaki the sandwiches she had brought along, and ate some herself. She supposed that the reason she felt not the least lonely at being separated from her husband today was that her present work was unquestionably for his sake, and this made the spiritual ties between them even stronger than when they were together. But of late the spiritual ties which Kazu was so fond of depicting to herself had come to exist only in her fantasies and her own interpretations.

Omé was an old-fashioned, quiet town spared by the war. Kazu stopped the car before the city hall, and, surrounded by reporters from the local newspapers, earlier alerted by Yamazaki, she proceeded to the mayor's office. She met the mayor and offered him her contribution for the war memorial. It was then decided that the assistant mayor and the dancing teacher from Kazu's part of the country would join Kazu in her car and direct her to the monument in Nagayama Park. The way led through the side streets of the town, took them north over a small land bridge, and finally climbed the gentle slope of an automobile road cut into the hill behind the town.

Kazu exclaimed in admiration at the beauty of the young leaves alongside the road. Wherever Kazu went she never forgot to praise the scenery. She considered this to be politically important. The politician's eye must find beauty everywhere in the landscape of his election districts; indeed, it takes a politician to appreciate nature's glories. He knows that each landscape is filled with a harvest of tempting and succulent fruits.

As expected, the view of the park on the hilltop captivated Kazu. She wept a little before the foundations of the monument to the war dead, and smiled a little to the women of the Folk Song Association who were gathered around the speakers' platform erected in the middle of an open space. But when she was led to a summerhouse set on a little elevation, the view from the top made her forget the press of everyday affairs.

The landscape unfolded to the southeast to reveal the gentle flow of the Tama River curving round east of the town, and glimpses of the broad river bed beyond the patches of forest shadows. The sweeping panorama was framed by the branches of the innumerable red pines in the park. The fuzzy young leaves on the mountains directly across the valley to the south glowed a saffron color. In spite of the radiance of the late afternoon sun, a haze lay everywhere, and the clumps of young leaves washed in the uncertain light looked as untidy as a woman's hair when she wakes in the morning. Kazu caught glimpses now and then of the bright colors of a bus flashing among the eaves of the town below.

"The scenery is lovely, isn't it?" she exclaimed. "What a wonderful view!"

"Yes," the assistant mayor said, "you won't find many views in the Tokyo region like the one from Nagayama Park." Then, using a map rolled around his hand to push aside the strings of festive paper lanterns hung from the eaves of the summerhouse to the branches of a nearby pine, he added, "That's the Tachikawa Base near the horizon to the east. It looks beautiful when you see it from here, at a distance."

Kazu turned her eyes in that direction. The course of the Tama River, exposed here and there at breaks in the woods, finally disappeared at the eastern end of the landscape, where a town white as rock salt glittered on the horizon. What she took at first for white chips bouncing into the sky were airplanes. Once they took off they flew low, level with the ground, and vanished into the shadows of the hills to the south. The whole area was so exceedingly white that Kazu thought it might be a cemetery. The Tachikawa Base seen from here did not suggest even remotely a town inhabited by human beings; it looked, rather, like a huge settlement of cold minerals poised at ground level. In the immense sky above drifted clouds of many shapes, hard and congealed the closer they were to the horizon, vaguer in outline higher up, until their form melted imperceptibly into smoke. Midway in the sky was a cluster of clouds glowing along its twisted upper edges, but revealing sculptural shadows below. Alone in this panorama the clouds seemed curiously unreal; they were like some marvelous lantern slide of clouds projected against the sky.

Thus a moment's light on a late spring afternoon created a strangely delicate yet certain landscape, never to be seen again. Even when the cypress forest in the foreground suddenly darkened, shaded by the clouds, the scenery on the horizon remained motionless, as though fastened in place.

Such a view did not, of course, suggest anything human to Kazu. She sensed the vast, beautiful, inorganic presence confronting her. Nature here bore no resemblance to the garden of the Setsugoan; it was not an exquisite, human miniature which she could hold in her hand. Yet, to gaze at this landscape was surely a political act. To gaze at it, sum it up, control it, was the work of politics.

Kazu's mind was not given to analysis, but the beauty instantly implanted in her eyes by this vista seemed to deny the political dreams she had entrusted to her ample flesh brimming with passion and tears, and to suggest with cruel mockery her unfitness for politics.

At that moment, as if she had just wakened from a dream, her ears caught the boom of a drum, the squawk of a record blared through a loudspeaker behind her, and then a chorus of many voices singing a folk song in time with the drum and the record. She noticed for the first time the garish colors of the ornamental lanterns hung everywhere. One string of lanterns wound over the tops of a row of maple trees, their branches of soft young leaves festooned at the tips with many small grape-colored flowers.

All of a sudden Kazu caught Yamazaki's hand. "Let's join them! Let's dance with them!" she cried, starting off.

"Well," said the assistant mayor, "this is certainly a surprise, Mrs. Noguchi."

Kazu's eyes were no longer on the scenery. She let the dancing teacher guide her into the crowd of folk dancers. The wives and daughters of the town, all in matching happi, were led by the members of the Folk Song Association in the singing of the *Kiso-bushi* as they danced. Kazu's hands automatically imitated the dancers' hands, and her feet as naturally followed.

"Clumsy, aren't you?" Kazu said, tapping Yamazaki's shoulder. He looked ungainly in a business suit, and kept confusing the movements of his hands and feet. "I'll stand in front and you follow me."

"You're a genius, Mrs. Noguchi," exclaimed the

teacher as they danced, "there's no need to give you instruction."

The assistant mayor stood outside the circle of dancers looking on in dumb surprise.

Before long the two citified newcomers, the only dancers not wearing happi, became the object of the others' attention. Kazu was already intoxicated. Perspiring freely in the bright sunlight, she melted into the human organism. She had only to brush against the bodies of the dancing women and smell their odor to forget at once her individuality and lose herself in the dance. She could feel no wall of any sort between herself and these strangers whose town she was visiting for the first time. The frantic beating of the drum on the platform and the piercing wail of the record were all Kazu's body needed to become one with the dancers; the perspiration which trickled an instant later down her cheeks was no longer hers alone.

As soon as the song came to an end Kazu turned to the assistant mayor. "I feel completely happy," she said. "I want to sing the *Sado Okesa* for everybody. There's a microphone on the stand, isn't there?"

A crowd of faces of village housewives gathered around Kazu. Most were past middle age, and looked as if they now enjoyed comfortable little incomes, but the sweat had ruined their holiday make-up and exposed leathery skins burnt by the sun of half a lifetime's labor. The small eyes bright with curiosity, the friendly gold-toothed smiles, the frizzy back hair—Kazu had absolute confidence before such faces.

The assistant mayor, making his way through the crowd, escorted Kazu onto the platform. The steps were steep, but a certain amount of danger of this kind made Kazu happy. The assistant mayor called into the microphone, "Ladies and gentlemen, we have with us today the wife of the famous statesman of the Radical Party, Yuken Noguchi. She has come all the way from Tokyo to see our Folk Song Festival. I'd like to ask Mrs. Noguchi to sing for us the *Sado Okesa*."

Kazu stepped up to the microphone and greeted the

crowd. "I am the wife of Yuken Noguchi. It has given me so much pleasure just to see you enjoy yourselves that I thought I'd like to sing you a song, if you'll pardon my voice. Please, everybody, dance as I sing."

Kazu clapped her hands to give the time to the young drummer. A general stir went through the crowd below, watching her, but once she began to sing it grew still, and then everybody started to dance as if loosened of all inhibitions.

*The trees and grasses all beckon to Sado, to Sado,
A good place to be, a good place to live is Sado.
I think of the past, then the tears wet my eyes—
Oh, Bay of Love on a night when the moon was misty!*

Kazu stayed until dusk, by turns climbing down from the platform to dance and climbing back to sing. Several women from the Folk Song Association went up on the platform with her and taught her one of the local ballads.

At dusk the lanterns strung on branches all over the park were lit simultaneously. Kazu, entreated to sing a third *Sado Okesa*, again climbed the platform alone. The blackness of the surrounding mountains seemed to close in on them, now that the lanterns were lit. When Kazu had finished the song applause echoed from the hillside, a rare occurrence at such a festival. Yamazaki excitedly climbed up to the platform. "You're a great success," he said into Kazu's ear. "The housewives of the Folk Song Association are saying that they won't let you leave tonight. You've conquered Santama at last."

"Do you think so?" Kazu asked, her eyes going out to the distant mountainside as she wiped the perspiration with a handkerchief.

"You must be tired."

"No, I don't feel too bad."

While Kazu had been singing this time, something on a mountainside across the valley had caught her attention. It was a point of fire, now visible, now vanishing, on the black surface of the mountain which seemed to close in with the coming night. Too feeble to be called a flame, it looked more like sparks thrown up now and then by a fire. Kazu could not remember having seen by day any houses in the fold in the mountains where the flame now rose, illuminated the area, then died out again. She looked carefully and noticed a trail of smoke extending diagonally upward to the ridge.

"What is that fire?" Kazu asked the young drummer. He had peeled off his shirt and was busy wiping the sweat.

"That fire?" he asked, turning to another young man. "What do you think it is?"

"That's the chimney of the municipal crematorium." The insolent looking, long-faced boy answered carelessly. Kazu remembered with feelings of sweetness Noguchi and the Noguchi family grave.

CHAPTER XII

COLLISION

The customers at the Setsugoan dwindled each day. First of all, Genki Nagayama stopped coming. The last time he appeared sparks had flown between him and Kazu when she visited his room.

"You certainly seem to be throwing yourself into the fray," Nagayama said, grinning.

"What would that refer to, I wonder?"

"But people are saying, 'The enemy is elsewhere.' "

"You talk more and more in riddles."

"All I mean to say is that you needn't go to such extremes just because you're in love with your husband."

"Really? I've always thought that when a woman fell in love she could even commit murder without any qualms."

"Murder could be forgiven. But there are worse things than murder. You've sold our tricks to the enemy."

"When have I ever sold any secret of yours?"

"I'm not talking about secrets. I'm talking about tricks. What you're doing now is to teach little baby Radical Party wicked tricks. The kind of wicked tricks which have always been our exclusive property."

"The tricks I learned from you don't amount to much."

"I suppose it'd be useless to try to stop you, with your nature. Go ahead, do what you please. But remember, violations of the election law by the Radical Party can't be overlooked. Be careful. Your pals can thank their stars they've never had any money before. That's what's kept them out of jail."

"Thank you for your kind advice. But don't forget, if

I'm caught I'll have quite a bit to tell the district attorney myself."

Nagayama colored, and he fell silent. Then, perhaps deciding that it would seem childish to stalk out of the party on the spot, he treated the other guests to a few of his usual dirty stories before leaving much sooner than his accustomed time. Kazu started to show him down the hall to the door when Nagayama, putting his arm around Kazu's shoulder, lightly patted her breasts. Such a dismal pretense at love-making irrevocably alienated Kazu from Nagayama.

The following day, when Yamazaki visited the Setsugoan at Kazu's request, he found her in her room. She was being massaged and wore only a thin undergarment. Yamazaki was dazzled by the superb pink of the underrobe, but he recognized at once that Kazu's slatternly pose, which might easily have been mistaken for enticement, represented the informality she permitted herself only with a man she did not love. The pink underrobe became disarranged as Kazu's hips were massaged, and Yamazaki caught a glimpse of her dazzlingly white thighs. The thighs had a glossy luminosity incredible in a woman in her middle fifties. Kazu felt no sense of responsibility about leaving her thighs exposed.

"What can I do for you?" Yamazaki demanded. "Please tell me quickly before I get the wrong ideas."

"Nothing special. I called you just to take a load off your mind." Kazu raised herself a little, rather warily, like a woman getting up on a rocking boat. "I'd like you to stop worrying. Whatever we do there's absolutely no danger of being arrested."

"What makes you so sure? That's the Committee Chairman's biggest worry."

"I did a little threatening, and now everything will be all right." Kazu, without listening to Yamazaki's reply, turned over on her stomach. As the masseur was rubbing her arm she added, "Now about that labor union dinner you requested the other day. I'll be glad to take it on, but please let me decide the cost."

"Thank you very much, but remember, they're not very well off."

"Surely they can afford 300 yen a head?"

"Three hundred yen?" The figure was so low Yamazaki was astonished.

"Yes, three hundred yen. I know we'll be needing their help more and more from now on, and I'd like to invite them without charge, but that would only burden them with feelings of obligation. Of course I'll provide the finest quality of food and drink."

Kazu gathered an unexpected harvest during the course of the conversation that day. She learned for the first time from some casual remarks made by Yamazaki, who assumed she already knew of the incident, that several months before the war ended Noguchi had petitioned the emperor to open peace negotiations. Kazu was overjoyed at this proof of Noguchi's enlightened views, and reproached Yamazaki for not having mentioned it before.

Kazu proposed that they immediately prepare a pamphlet utilizing this information, but Yamazaki hesitated to do so without Noguchi's knowledge. Yet if they revealed their project to Noguchi he would be certain to express his unalterable opposition. Kazu's determination to carry through her scheme without informing Noguchi suggested that she now recognized no restraints.

She spoke fluently. "There's no need, of course, to consult with my husband. We couldn't hope for better material. It's obvious that our only possible reason for using it is to help him, and we'd be guilty of negligence, wouldn't we, if we allowed such valuable material to lie idle."

In the end Yamazaki was talked into consenting. Kazu also got him to agree to a marvelous plan she had thought up one sleepless night—to print 500,000 calendars with Noguchi's photograph. Each calendar would cost about four yen, and they would have to have a stylish design. The calendars would be distributed to all labor unions, and through the teachers' union would find their way to the walls of the pupils' homes.

Kazu described to Yamazaki the full range of her fancy, forgetting as usual the passage of time . . . The calendars would be hung on factory walls, next to seamstresses' sewing machines, in children's study rooms. Noguchi's name would come up in family conversations even at the dinner table. "Who's that man on the calendar?" "Yuken Noguchi, of course. Don't you know about him?" . . . His photograph would always be smiling! His photograph, graced by his dignified, elderly gentleman's smile, must watch benevolently over many scantily laid dinner tables and accept cheerfully on its face the steam rising from the dishes. The calendar must steal in everywhere—by the bird cage, under the old wall clock, beside the television set, just above the little kitchen blackboard with its shopping list of vegetables and fish, next to the cupboard where the family cat sleeps—and Noguchi's smile must hover over all. Then his silver-haired dignity and his smile must cause him to merge imperceptibly in voters' minds with dear old uncles who many years ago brought them candy and stroked their heads whenever he visited the house. The smile must confuse memories, revive old, heavily romantic dreams of justice triumphant, and, as the name of an old ship in the harbor becomes a synonym for the future when it sets sail, his name must become another name for a future which would see wretched, smoke-stained walls battered down.

"When," Kazu pursued, "the family cat gets up and stretches, it will rub its back against Noguchi's face on the calendar. Then, as the old gentleman of the house picks up the cat, he'll see the smile on Noguchi's face. Never will his expression look so dear, so indulgent as it does at that moment."

As Yamazaki was leaving, Kazu whispered one final bit of information. "You don't need to worry about money. I've mortgaged the Setsugoan. Tomorrow I'll have at my disposal about twenty-five million yen."

The Radical Party and the labor unions were experienced when it came to elections with up to 300,000 votes, but they had no idea of the proper strategy when it came to an electorate of five million; they were in fact completely bewildered. Word to this effect from Yamazaki had inspired Kazu with greater confidence than ever. She came to think that the election was her Heaven-appointed task. It was a game in which one used one's full energies against a virtual vacuum for an adversary, a constant wager directed against something whose existence could not be verified. She felt that however excited she became, she could never be excited enough, that however dispassionate she acted, she could never be dispassionate enough, and there was no standard by which to judge either. Kazu was exempt from one worry, the fear that she might be going too far. Yamazaki was no match for her in this. The time-tested veteran of Radical Party elections had gradually developed into an admirer of the grand-scale methods which Kazu invariably adopted.

One dark day of unbroken rain Kazu, returning to the Setsugoan toward evening, noticed one of her trusted maids standing at the inside entrance, a look of distress on her face. "Mr. Noguchi is here," she said.

"Where is he?"

"He's waiting in your room, ma'am."

"What made you take him to such a place?"

"He came here a while ago without any warning, and walked straight to your room himself."

Kazu stood rooted to the spot. This was Noguchi's first unannounced visit to the Setsugoan. What sent chills through her was the recollection that the room adjacent to hers was filled with enormous stacks of calendars and pamphlets just off the press.

Her heart beating like a trip hammer, Kazu stood motionless, unable even to remove her wet raincoat. She sensed the dreadful expression her face must present in the hallway light. The old porter, who had accompanied Kazu from the gate, protecting her with an umbrella, stared at her face, forgetting to close his umbrella.

Every conceivable variety of falsehood suggested itself to Kazu. A genius for cheerful evasion was part of her natural endowments, and however serious the predicament facing her, she could always manage to dodge it nimbly, like a swallow threading a narrow path under projecting eaves. In this instance, however, she felt that silence would be the best evasion. There was no doubt about her basic good intentions, and basically she had nothing to feel ashamed of. But Kazu feared Noguchi more than anything else in the world.

As Kazu slowly removed her coat she glanced back at the rain pouring down on the path between the gate and the inside entrance. The driving rain was battering the vermilion pomegranate flowers. Spring was warmer this year than usual, and the flowers had opened very early. Their flame color continued to glow intensely in the approaching darkness outside. The flowers calmed Kazu somewhat.

She kneeled at the threshold of her room. "I'm sorry I was out when you came," she said.

Noguchi, in Japanese clothes, got up without answering. All but kicking Kazu out of the room with his outstretched foot, he barked, "We're going home at once. Come!" He strode out into the hallway. Kazu noticed that he had a pamphlet and a folded calendar in his right hand. As Noguchi crossed over the humped bridge of the passageway ahead of her, she suddenly recalled the same view of him the night of their first meeting, and she felt a rush of mingled sadness and affection. It seemed then that all she had done entirely of her own volition was actually the working of an unhappy destiny. She wept as she followed him.

The maids, long accustomed to Kazu's tears, showed no suspicion that anything was amiss even when she weepingly left the Setsugoan. Noguchi's mouth was set in an obdurate line. Kazu continued to weep in the car all the way home, but Noguchi did not utter a single word.

When they were back in the house Noguchi, still without a word, led Kazu into his study and locked the door. There was nothing of fire about his anger; it rose like a steep unsurmountable precipice. "Do you know why I went to the Setsugoan?" he demanded.

Kazu, still weeping, shook her head faintly. A trace of

coquetry flickered in her attitude as she shook her head, though she herself disapproved of it. The next instant Noguchi slapped her in the face. She collapsed on the carpet and wept.

"Do you understand now?" Noguchi shouted, breathing heavily. "Today there was a telephone call at the house from the printers. I answered it. They said that the bill for the calendars hadn't been paid, and they wanted their money. They informed me that my wife had ordered the calendars. I asked a few questions. I discovered that it was your doing. Then I went to the Setsugoan, and what did I find? Not only calendars! What is the meaning of this? What intolerable impertinence!"

Noguchi struck Kazu's face again and again with the pamphlet. She had often enough had arguments with her husband, but never before anything like this. Even as she felt the sting of his blows, she stole an upward glance at him. Noguchi was breathing heavily, but his face was not distorted by anger. The coldness of his fury made Kazu tremble.

"You've smeared mud on your husband's face. Just the kind of thing I could expect of you. You've done a wonderful job of besmirching my career. You should be ashamed of yourself, yes, ashamed! Does it make you happy that your husband's become a public laughing stock?"

He stamped on Kazu's body as she lay on the floor, anywhere his feet happened to land, but his frail body was strengthless. Kazu rolled over shrieking, but his feet were in fact repulsed by the rich resilience of her body. Noguchi finally settled himself in a chair on the other side of his desk, and distantly regarded Kazu lying sobbing on the floor.

Noguchi's denunciation, antiquated both in manner and language, intensified his aura of being the incarnation of the old moral virtues. His wrath was cast in a majestic idiom which delighted Kazu; all but swooning from pain and happiness, she deliberately reflected with her half-conscious faculties that Noguchi was the kind of man who, once he had angrily forbidden whatever deserved to be forbidden, would immediately revert to his normal blindness and deafness. This reflection, many times repeated, made Kazu indulgent again toward Noguchi, and even more so toward herself.

Kazu, howling like some wild beast, begged for forgiveness, and shrieked every imaginable excuse. She would grow calm, apparently losing consciousness, only to howl for forgiveness again, her voice louder than ever. Noguchi prolonged the torture, declaring that he would not let her out of the room until she confessed everything, it being evident that she had spent a considerable amount of money. Kazu babbled incoherently, "Money I saved myself . . . I used it for your sake . . . All for your sake. . . ."

Noguchi listened coldly to these protestations. Then, by way of indicating his refusal to pay attention to a word of her excuses, he took a German book from the shelf and, turning from Kazu, began to read.

A fairly long silence ensued. The room was dark save for the circle of light cast by the desk lamp. All that could be heard, apart from the sound of the rain and the occasional rustle when Noguchi turned a page of his book, was Kazu's agitated breathing. The plump, middle-aged woman sprawled on the floor, the hems of her kimono twisted, was the only jarring note in this quiet evening in the study. Kazu was aware that her thighs were visible through her skirts, and that they rose and fell slightly with her breathing at the outer edge of the dim lamplight. She knew with certainty which parts of her flesh were exposed by the chill gradually numbing them. She pitied their undeniable futility, and knew by their coldness and numbness that the faintly discernible white parts of her thighs were being subjected to a total rejection. She felt as if Noguchi's rejection flowed through their numbness into her body.

Kazu at last rearranged her disordered costume, sat properly, and touching her hands to the carpet in a deep bow, declared that she would confess everything. She held nothing back from Noguchi, even to her mortgaging the Setsugoan.

Noguchi said in a surprisingly gentle voice, "There's no helping what's already been done. But you are to shut the Setsugoan as of tomorrow, and from now on you will live here all the time. You follow me, I trust? Remember, you're not to set foot out of the house!"

"Shut the Setsugoan?"

"Yes. If you think I'm asking too much, I'll have no choice but to divorce you."

This threat frightened Kazu more than a beating. A great, dark hole opened before her eyes. "If he divorces me, there'll be nobody to look after my grave when I'm dead. . . ." At this thought Kazu made up her mind to pay any compensation Noguchi might exact.

CHAPTER XIII

AN OBSTACLE IN THE PATH
OF LOVE

Kazu concluded, as the result of this quarrel, that she had no choice but to offer the Setsugoan for sale. The Setsugoan had already occasioned gossip, and was likely to be used as material for counter-propaganda. As far as Noguchi was concerned, it could only be considered the base of his wife's undesirable activities. It enraged Noguchi that Kazu had mortgaged the Setsugoan without telling him, and used the money to finance the pre-election campaign. He had come to think that the best thing would be to extirpate the roots of evil by placing the Setsugoan on sale, and then use the money fairly and squarely to meet election expenses. Noguchi had learned for the first time how poor the party was.

The disposal of the Setsugoan was left to Noguchi. Kazu had a fierce attachment for the Setsugoan, and words could not describe her grief at relinquishing it, but in the end she preferred to a beautiful garden the small, moss-encrusted tomb of the Noguchi family.

The complications of the sale, however, unexpectedly provided Kazu with a splendid excuse for escaping from confinement in Noguchi's house and returning to the Setsugoan. Once back there, Kazu did absolutely nothing about liquidating the affairs of the restaurant. Her employees were uneasy about the protracted closing, but she kept them in ignorance of the impending sale. Safe in her retreat at the Setsugoan, she would daily summon Yamazaki and examine with him stratagems of every kind. When a good plan suggested itself, she was so excited she could hardly sit still, and she would immediately order her car to get ready. Thus, despite the severe reprimand she had received, everything in Kazu's life—save for the closing of the Setsugoan—reverted to normal.

Noguchi had requested a lawyer, a close friend of his, to arrange the sale, and before long a promising buyer turned up, Genzo Fujikawa of Fujikawa Associates. His counsel entered into negotiations with Noguchi's lawyer, and it seemed as though a quick settlement was in the offing. The other party, however, refused to budge an inch beyond an offer of eighty million yen toward the asking price of one hundred million.

Kazu happened to be at the Setsugoan one day when the maid announced a telephone call from Genki Nagayama. As far as she was concerned, she had broken relations with Nagayama, and she felt no inclination to go to the telephone. But Yamazaki, who was sitting beside her, urged her with a little push to answer.

Kazu, despite her promise to obey Yamazaki's directions to the letter, was annoyed at this instance of his interference, and at the touch of his hand on her knee she recoiled a foot or two over the tatami. The leopard-like resilience of her comfortable plump flesh made Yamazaki stare in astonishment. Kazu kept her head obstinately averted, her eyes on the garden soaked by the spring rains. The garden was a green blur.

"What makes you get angry? All I did was to suggest that you answer the phone. I think you should."

Kazu did not reply. She had remembered Nagayama's thick, olive-brown lips. Nagayama suddenly seemed like the embodiment of all the mud of half a lifetime. This thickset, power-saturated man resembled all the memories most painful to a woman. Even her refusal ever to have relations with Nagayama, her having been treated like a sister, originally stemmed mainly from tarnished self-esteem. However severely Noguchi reviled her, Kazu could always preserve her integrity, but one grin from Nagayama and she felt as if the depths of her being had been laid bare ... Kazu, in short, disliked her momentary feelings of relief when informed at this juncture of a call from Nagayama.

She rose and slipped off to her own room, where she had the call transferred. She said "hello" into the receiver, all but enfolding it with her body, and the secretary's voice was presently replaced by Nagayama's.

"What's happened? You're still annoyed with me, is that it? Well, you can snub me all you please, I still consider myself your lifelong friend. I hear, by the way, that you've finally got around to closing the Setsugoan. But you'll still serve me a cup of tea and some biscuits, won't you? We're still pals, after all."

"If I make exceptions, even for one person, the place isn't closed anymore."

"I see. Do you intend giving up the restaurant and opening a special-service bathhouse for the working class—is that it?"

"That would suit me. The younger and livelier the customers, the better."

"That's funny. I thought your husband's age was pretty close to mine."

"I've had enough of your offensive remarks. What did you say your business was?"

"Nothing special. I just wondered if we couldn't have lunch together for a change."

Kazu refused point-blank, explaining that she was no longer at liberty to do so. In that case, Nagayama said, there was no helping it, he would tell her over the phone. He then quite nonchalantly broached a most unexpected and important matter.

"That stone head of Noguchi's is giving us a lot of trouble. I sent a man to Noguchi—no doubt you know all about this—with an offer to withdraw the opposing candidate on the condition that if elected Noguchi would choose someone from the Conservative Party as his lieutenant governor. What could be more generous than that? But Noguchi, as usual, stubbornly refused to listen.

It's entirely to his advantage, and as long as he accepts that one condition, he's sure to be elected. I trust you'll advise him strongly to accept . . . I should warn you of something. If Noguchi turns down the offer, you'll probably find you have trouble selling the Setsugoan. I'm telling you this entirely for your own good."

At this point Kazu hurriedly cut the conversation short. Her walk as she returned along the corridor to the room where she had left Yamazaki betrayed her agitation. Yamazaki could tell merely from the sound of her footsteps that Kazu was angry.

Kazu slid the door shut behind her and, still standing, angrily exclaimed, "Mr. Yamazaki—how could you be so cruel? To think that an important offer's been made to my husband, and you've never even breathed a word!"

Kazu's thin eyebrows stood on end when she was angry, and her mouth turned down in a frown. Her obi, tied somewhat low, presented a hard, flat, domineering surface, an impression strengthened by her practice of tying the sash band squarely in front in a countrified style, instead of at a more fashionable angle.

"Please sit down," Yamazaki said. He patiently explained the situation to Kazu, who sat facing sideways, her head obstinately turned away from him, like a small child. It would only have confused her, he said, if they had told Kazu of the offer, and the right course for her, in any case, was to devote her full energies to the campaign. Noguchi had refused even to consider the honeyed words of the Conservative Party, and if it were a proposal worthy of his consideration, it would be more effective for the party leaders to suggest this than his wife. The present telephone call had delighted Yamazaki because it showed that Kazu's pre-election campaign was developing into a threat to the enemy. The Conservatives had put up a candidate named Gen Tobita, a desperate choice in whom the Conservative Party itself had no confidence, as the telephone call just now demonstrated. The reluctance of the present governor of the prefecture to resign, though he had long seemed on the point, was owing to the Conservative Party's failure to obtain the Prime Minister's endorsement for their candidate. It was a pity that Noguchi did not make political capital out of the offer, but as far as Kazu was concerned, the most important thing was not to become rattled: it was now clear that her efforts were bearing fruit.

Yamazaki applied himself with painstaking care to the explanation. Kazu's face suddenly shone like the garden in the first rays of the morning sun. Yamazaki, looking on her miraculously transformed face, thought it beautiful. It was as if a smiling face, complete to the last detail, had unexpectedly surfaced from under her other face, revealing in its new-born freshness not the faintest trace of the raging emotions of the moment before.

"You don't say!" she cried. "Well, this calls for a celebration! Tonight I'll drink a toast with you!" Kazu stood and, throwing open the sliding doors, danced into the adjoining banqueting hall. At the other end of the room stood a beautiful screen painting by Tatebayashi Kagei depicting in the manner of Korin a curved bridge over a silvery stream and ranks of irises. Kazu opened the banqueting hall shoji facing the garden, and Yamazaki saw now a green corner contiguous to the wet landscape visible from the small room where he sat.

Now that the Setsugoan was closed, it looked even lovelier in the early twilight of a rainy day than when filled with noisy guests. The chilly gloom of the banqueting hall actually lent greater resplendence to the lacquered furniture and painted screens. Kazu appeared to Yamazaki, looking at her from behind, to have become half a shadow picture, but she so overflowed with vitality that she seemed to have gathered into herself all the life which once filled this huge, empty room.

Kazu stepped onto the veranda and, looking out on the garden, caught the door frame with the toes of her white-encased feet, like a parrot on a perch, and balanced herself precariously. The action had no particular meaning, but she remained on her uncertain roost.

She stared at her toes. They stood out white and distinct between the dimness of the room and the hazy green outside, firmly curled, like an intelligent little animal. She spread open her toes. The shining wrinkles bulged in her tabi. Then the strain of being supported only by her toes in this unsteady posture spread through her body, bringing with it a kind of pleasurable sensation of danger. Just a little relaxation of the tension and her body would tumble onto the wet shrubs and the garden stones, and sink into the rain-soaked greenery.

Yamazaki, stepping into the banqueting room, noticed Kazu's body teetering back and forth in a strangely unnerving manner. He rushed up in alarm, calling, "Is there anything wrong, Mrs. Noguchi?"

Kazu turned round and laughed aloud, showing her teeth. "What an awful thing to say! I'm not old enough yet for apoplexy! I was just amusing myself . . . But it's time now for our drinking."

Kazu and Yamazaki made the rounds of the bars and cabarets. Yamazaki could not help noticing out of the corner of his eye, even in his drunkenness, that Kazu was busily distributing the extra-large visiting cards, even to the waitresses and bus boys.

Noguchi bluntly rejected the compromise plan offered him by the Conservative Party through two or three devious channels. Several days later the counsel for Fujikawa Associates abruptly informed Noguchi's lawyer that he could not agree to the terms for the sale of the Setsugoan. Noguchi's lawyer discovered on investigation that pressure applied by Prime Minister Saeki was responsible for this new development. The Prime Minister, it was understood, had made a sudden telephone call to Genzo Fujikawa: "This is no time to buy the Setsugoan. It's putting ammunition in the enemy's hands, just before an election."

Noguchi was furious at the report. Yamazaki, who never got angry, declared that they now had a favorable opportunity to engage the enemy, and after urging Noguchi at some length, arranged for a public interview with the Prime Minister.

Noguchi called on Saeki, his junior in years, at the

official residence. In his usual pompous, awkward phraseology he condemned the Prime Minister for his underhanded interference in the settlement of a private transaction. The Prime Minister, smiling, protested deferentially that he had absolutely no recollection of such an occurrence. "Besides, I find the story a little too dramatic to be believable. Does it seem reasonable that the prime minister of a nation would make a telephone call like some cheap broker? Please use your common sense. I wonder if the simplest explanation isn't that Fujikawa used my name in order to furnish himself with a plausible excuse for refusing?"

Saeki treated Noguchi like an extremely old man, all but offering his hand to help him sit down or get up from his chair, wounding the pride of the old diplomat by such excessive politeness. True finesse requires a silken touch, but Saeki's at best was rayon. "What does the little trickster think he's doing?" Noguchi thought.

Kazu sensed Noguchi's bad humor when he returned, and comforted him without saying a word. It was hopeless now to try to sell the Setsugoan. Kazu did her best to hide her joy. She decided that she would have to make up for the treachery of her emotions by her political fidelity.

CHAPTER XIV

THE ELECTION AT LAST

The governor of the prefecture resigned from office in the last week of July, and an election was immediately proclaimed. The fifteen days up to the tenth of August was the period sanctioned for campaigning. It was an extremely hot summer. Kazu, strenuously active again, took a second mortgage on the Setsugoan and raised thirty million yen. An election office was opened on the second floor of a downtown building.

She and Noguchi had another altercation on the long-awaited morning of the election proclamation, just as Noguchi was about to leave the house to deliver his first campaign address. Kazu had, in anticipation of this day, purchased summer suiting of the finest English material, and had been at great pains to get a tailor to take her husband's measurements. Noguchi, however, disliked the suit. He intended to deliver his first street address wearing a linen suit which had turned completely yellow with age.

"I am standing for office as Yuken Noguchi, and not as a tailor's dummy," he announced. "I can't wear such a thing."

Such childish drivel, as anyone could see, covered an undercurrent of narrow-minded dread. Who in his audience seeing the old man's new suit would conceivably guess that his wife had provided it? Even Yamazaki had said, "He's just acting like a spoiled child for your benefit, Mrs. Noguchi. Don't worry about him.

Just order the suit to the measurements of his old clothes."

Kazu was not one to place much reliance on divine help in times of need, but that morning she rose at four and lit a candle before the Buddhist altar. She had decided to persuade the late Mrs. Noguchi to join their cause and cooperate in the interest of a Noguchi victory. Mosquitoes drifted in from the pre-dawn darkness of the garden and circled round Kazu's hands when she joined them in prayer. There was no trace of piety in her tone as she silently addressed the late Mrs. Noguchi. "What do you say? Let's join hands, one woman to another, and help him win somehow." Kazu felt as if a beautiful friendship for this woman she had never met was rapidly materializing, and she wept a little. "What a fine lady, a fine lady. I am sure that if you were still alive we'd become good friends!"

The mosquitoes repeatedly stung Kazu's mellow flesh. She felt as though it would somehow help Noguchi to win if she could endure the itching. In this manner Kazu communed for quite a long time with the late Sadako Noguchi.

In the meantime, sunrise brought the first intense light of the summer day to the garden. The garden was full of trees, and the sunlight shining through the stencils of leaf clusters stamped complicated shadows like paper cutouts in the center of the garden. Glancing over her shoulder at the garden stones, now a shining white, Kazu felt as if an auspicious crane had glided down through the sunrise: the stones suggested a crane with outstretched wings. She remembered now—when was it?—telling Noguchi as a joke that a crane was flying over the garden, and it had proved no lie. To see a crane now was indeed a lucky sign, but fearing Noguchi's rebuke, she decided not to tell him.

Noguchi woke soon afterward and took breakfast with Kazu, his usual silent ritual.

"Wouldn't you like a raw egg?" Kazu finally asked.

He bluntly refused. "I'm not taking part in a grammar school athletic meet." Noguchi was extremely vain about his unexcitability, presumably a product of his English training, but he completely lacked the sardonic, sophisticated humor which in an Englishman reinforces this detachment. Noguchi deliberately acted disagreeable that morning in order to prove that he was maintaining his usual calm.

Yamazaki arrived, followed by the people from campaign headquarters. Kazu, as previously arranged, brought forward in Yamazaki's presence the new summer suit in a clothes box and a white rose. Noguchi gave the clothes box a glance and said, "What's this? You don't expect me to wear such clothes?" Kazu, though resolved not to become emotional, wanted so badly to have her wishes gratified that she burst into tears. Noguchi for his part grew only the more obstinate, and Yamazaki, interceding, attempted to mollify him. At last Noguchi grudgingly tried on the new coat, but he absolutely rejected the flower pinned to the lapel.

The time for Noguchi's departure had come, and everyone went to the door to see him off. Kazu was moved to see Noguchi's immaculate shirt and new suit. When she reached out her hand to straighten his collar though it did not need straightening, Noguchi with extraordinary alertness gripped her right hand firmly but inconspicuously. Even an acute observer might have interpreted this as a gesture of reserved affection, but Noguchi said in a low voice, "Stop your foolishness. It's disgraceful."

Noguchi's sharp, bony fingers snatched away in an instant's scuffle the objects Kazu kept tightly concealed in the palm of her right hand. They were flint stones for stricking good-luck sparks. Kazu knew how much her husband disliked such customs, but she could not resist her impulse to strike sparks for her husband's departure before the others. Noguchi had unerringly guessed that she had the stones hidden in her hand.

Once in the car Noguchi silently passed the stones to Yamazaki for his safekeeping. Yamazaki was surprised, but immediately guessed what had happened. He was bothered the whole of the busy day by the stones rolling around in his pocket.

Noguchi went to the Prefectural Office, filed notice of his intention of standing for election, received a sash with his name written on it, then left immediately for the open-air meeting area at the Yaesu Entrance to Tokyo Station. The nine o'clock sunlight of a summer morning glared on the white shirts of the crowd already gathered in the square. Many held fans over their heads to protect them from the sun. Noguchi stepped from his car, and was politely greeted by the officials of the labor unions and supporting groups who had been waiting for him near the loudspeaker truck. Noguchi climbed up the rear of the truck. He announced, without the least trace of affability, "I am Yuken Noguchi, the Radical Party candidate in the gubernatorial election." He then launched into a long enumeration of his idealistic policies delivered in an absolutely colorless voice. In the midst of a sentence the microphone suddenly went dead. Noguchi, not realizing that the microphone had ceased to function, continued with his address. At that precise moment the opposing candidate, Gen Tobita, began his address at the other end of the square. His microphone blasted out his ringing voice so efficiently that even those standing in the front ranks of Noguchi's listeners were deafened by Tobita's voice denouncing Noguchi and the Radical Party. It seemed improbable that Noguchi's microphone could be repaired immediately, and it was therefore decided to return temporarily to campaign headquarters before starting out afresh for the Koto District. There was no denying that this was an unpromising start.

Noguchi's first speech had disappointed his young supporters. "I wonder if the old man couldn't put a little more feeling into his words," Yamazaki heard one say at headquarters, and then another: "The immediate abolition of horse racing and bicycle racing is all well and good, but it wasn't very clever of him to come out with it right at the beginning."

Kazu's speeches, on the other hand, were the incarnation of feeling, and wherever she went she was showered with applause by audiences listening half with amusement. In the end she delivered a thirty-minute address in the glaring afternoon sunlight of the square before Shibuya Station. A bucket of cracked ice stood at Kazu's feet, and she frequently wiped her face with a handkerchief full of ice. She spoke in a loud voice, her mouth too close to the microphone, making it difficult for her words to be understood, but she delighted her audience with her passionate, auction-room delivery. Kazu brought up the matter of Noguchi's memorial to the emperor, using the following line of argument. "I am the wife of Yuken Noguchi. Yet, though I am the wife of Yuken Noguchi, my husband Mr. Noguchi never told even told me, his wife, about this memorial. That shows how reluctant a man he is to boast about his achievements. But I can tell you that when I learned the truth of the matter, I was astonished. I hope you will pardon me for mentioning it, ladies and gentlemen, but it is really largely thanks to Mr. Noguchi that all of us, and I include myself, are able today to go about our daily business peacefully. Yes, I was astonished to think of it. Mr. Noguchi was praying for peace all along . . ."

A young fellow on the street heckled her, "Don't brag so much about your husband!"

Kazu answered the heckler, "Yes, of course I'm bragging about my husband. I hope you'll let me brag about him. I guarantee you, as his wife, that if you vote for Noguchi you'll never regret it." Such exchanges earned her applause. The speech rambled on, with no end in sight, Kazu showing a stately indifference to the frantic signals flashed by the people in charge. Finally one young party worker, unable to bear any more, snatched the microphone away from Kazu. The make-up had been washed from her face by the applications of ice, revealing her healthy, north-country fair complexion. A blush spread over her face now, and an expression of violent anger, hitherto reserved for the maids at the Setsugoan—and Yamazaki—was displayed before the crowd. Kazu, stamping furiously on the floorboards of the sound truck, screamed, "What do you mean taking away the microphone? Do you want to kill Noguchi—is that it?"

The young party worker, alarmed, returned the microphone, and Kazu resumed, talking again at inordinate length. Kazu's passing fury afforded the crowd a magnificent spectacle. The moment when her face, shining bright red in the late afternoon sun and glittering with drops of ice, was transfigured with rage in the eyes of the large crowd, there was an instant of dead silence. People felt they had seen her naked.

Kazu's long orations ended, however, the first day. The exasperated party workers at campaign headquarters requested Kazu through Yamazaki henceforth to confine her speeches to half a page, or in time, to one minute. Her self-indulgent gushing over personal emotions was also restricted. There was a danger that if her emotions were allowed free course, they might easily wash away prefectural reform and democracy too.

Committee Chairman Kusakari, Chief Secretary Kimura, and Executive Director Kurosawa traveled throughout the prefecture giving speeches, following the schedule laid down by Campaign Headquarters—that is, Yamazaki. Noguchi delivered speech after speech, in the morning at selected strategic spots, in the afternoon at specified locations, and at night at campaign meetings and dinners. He appealed for support even to groups of day laborers and to fishermen on the wharfs. A "spy car" of the other party trailed Noguchi's truck on his far-flung peregrinations, always just out of sight, and a spy car from the Radical Party similarly followed Gen Tobita's public-address truck.

Kazu spent the whole day racing around in typical fashion, her bucketful of cracked ice beside her in the car, aiming at places where her husband was unlikely to be.

On the morning of the third day the loudspeaker truck stopped at a place on Kagurazaka Rise. Various party orators delivered addresses, and then Kazu stepped forward to make her one-minute speech. A face in the crowd of thirty or forty, a middle-aged man's, filled her heart with terror.

The summer sun beat mercilessly on the steeply sloping road. Few working men were to be seen in the faces upturned toward the campaign orators on the truck. The crowd consisted mainly of old people, housewives returning from shopping, children and students. The truck had pulled over to the shade and stopped there, but the spectators overflowed into the sunshine, some covering their heads with handkerchiefs. The Radical Party attracted simple, decent-looking audiences everywhere. The sunlight reflecting from their clear white summer shirts deepened this impression. Most of the time the crowd jostling under the truck was distinguished by rows of white teeth smiling under straw hats, by schoolgirls with glowing, downy faces untouched by cosmetics, and, in general, by arms and necks burnt a healthy tan by outdoor work. Kazu liked such listeners.

The middle-aged man she had noticed in the crowd, however, wore a grimy, wrinkled, open-collared shirt with two fountain-pen clips glittering in the breast pocket. His hands propped an old brief case against his chest, and a cigarette dangled between the fingers of one hand. He was hatless, and the fierce sunlight shining on his closely cropped gray-white hair made him twist his mouth into a smirk. Kazu took a moment to recognize him because of the short haircut. His features were above average, but old and faded, with the peculiar unpleasantness of the face of a handsome man who has gone to seed without losing his looks.

Kazu as usual began her speech with, "I am the wife of Yuken Noguchi." She felt as if the man were grinning at her. She finished her one-minute address, and the student volunteers thanked the audience for its kind attention. The crowd started to disperse and the truck prepared to leave for the next speaking engagement. At that moment Kazu saw the man stretch out his hand and rap against the side of the truck.

"Mrs. Noguchi!" the man called, baring his nicotine-stained teeth in a smile. "Mrs. Noguchi!"

Kazu immediately got down from the truck and approached the man. Her heart was throbbing strangely under the towel she had inserted in the breast of her kimono to catch the perspiration. She raised her voice deliberately. "Well! I haven't seen you in years. It really is a small world, isn't it? But what a surprising place for you to find me!"

She remembered his name—Totsuka—perfectly, but she prudently avoided mentioning it. She narrowed her eyes as if the sunlight were too much for her, but actually to keep her uneasiness from showing. She could see the train going over the elevated tracks at Sakashita. The few clouds in the sky had been melted by the sun into vague blobs.

"What do you want?" Kazu asked in a low voice.

"I'd like to talk with you for a minute," the man answered.

Kazu cheerfully called to the people on the truck, "I've met an old acquaintance, and I'd like a few words with him. Would you mind resting a minute or two, please?"

Kazu walked diagonally across the street and, intending that Totsuka should accompany her, marched into a sherbet parlor. The blue and white curtains of glass beads at the entrance looked cheerful enough, but the interior of the shop with its row of battered chairs was gloom itself. No sooner did Kazu set foot in the shop than she called in a loud voice, "Twenty sherbets for the people on the truck! Right away!" Then, "Two orders of sherbet here. Serve us after the others. Take the orders out to the truck as soon as they're ready."

Kazu and the man sat at a dark table under a calendar. The table was wet from the ices slopped over by the previous customer. Kazu had a sudden intuition, though she knew it was impossible, that the calendar above her head was graced with Noguchi's photograph. She looked up. She saw a movie actress in a yellow bathing suit floating in the water on blue-spotted water wings.

"What do you want?" Kazu asked again, impatient to be freed of her uncertainties.

"Don't be in such a hurry. I've got to hand it to you, all the same, the way you're going at it in this broiling weather. Your speech was damned good. Years ago I predicted that one day you'd be famous."

"Out with it, if you've something you want from me. Money, is it?" Kazu addressed this man she had not seen in thirty years with brutal directness. Her eyes flashed feverishly as she watched Totsuka's every move. The only sounds inside the shop was the steady rumble of the machine shaving the ice.

"Not very friendly, are you? To tell the truth, I've been doing a bit of writing recently." Totsuka ran his spread-out fingers over the old brief case and, after much fumbling, opened the bag. It was stuffed with wrinkled papers. Totsuka peered inside and searched for an interminable length of time. Reflections from the sunlight falling on the tiled floor at the entrance caught Totsuka's exceptionally long eyelashes as he looked down into the brief case. He had been proud of his long lashes when he was young, Kazu remembered. Now they shone an ashen color, but with their same remarkably lyrical beauty, shaded his wrinkle-set eyes.

"Ah, here we are," Totsuka said, pulling out a flimsy pamphlet and throwing it carelessly on the table. The cover was inscribed, "The Life of Mrs. Yuken Noguchi. By a Frolicsome Angler."

Kazu's hand trembled violently as she turned the pages. Each chapter bore a suggestive heading. The parts dealing with the youthful Kazu's arrival in Tokyo and her several years together with Totsuka described Totsuka (under his real name) as a handsome young man of pure and guileless emotions, and Kazu as a nymphomaniac. But, the book declared, it was her fixed policy, when there was a choice between love and ambition, to throw love to the winds and set her course for ambition. Each of her subsequent affairs was chronicled, with detailed excursions into the successive bedchambers. Kazu was pictured as nothing less than a vampire, trading on her beauty, who used men as stepping stones to her present position. As Kazu leafed rapidly through the last chapter she suddenly realized the purpose of the pamphlet. There she found Noguchi described as angelically naïve, and herself as an unscrupulous monster who had hoodwinked Noguchi and was now trying to be installed as the governor's wife.

Kazu, dry-eyed, whispered, "How dare you write such irresponsible lies?"

"Nobody knows but you and me whether they're lies or not." Totsuka's words, delivered with another flash of his stained teeth, were so reminiscent of the stereotype blackmailer in an old-fashioned melodrama that they suggested he need not be taken too seriously. Kazu, reassured, felt emboldened for the first time to look Totsuka in the face. Under her stare he dropped his long eyelashes. He's afraid too, Kazu thought.

The waitress brought the ices.

"Have some," Kazu haughtily commanded. The man, protecting the mound of shaved ice with one hand, mashed it down with his spoon, then thrust his mouth against the ice so as not to spill a drop. His long fingernails were rimmed with black dirt.

"Well, what's your price?" Kazu demanded cuttingly.

Totsuka quickly lifted his face from the ices. His eyes had a puppy's innocence. He pulled out a scrap of paper with some fussy calculations. Three thousand copies at three hundred yen a copy came to 900,000 yen, but he had rounded it off a bit to make a million yen.

"Very well. Come to my house tomorrow morning at ten o'clock. But you won't get a penny if I find that even one of the three thousand copies is missing. I'll pay you cash on delivery for all three thousand."

The next morning Kazu withdrew the money from the bank and waited for Totsuka. She turned over the money as promised when he appeared, then decided to wait until she had calmed down before burning the three thousand copies of the pamphlet she collected. She had them securely wrapped and thrown into the storeroom. Pleading an indisposition, she excused herself from speechmaking that morning and said nothing, even to Yamazaki, of what had happened.

Several days later, in spite of all promises, the scurrilous pamphlet was distributed free of charge to well-known persons throughout the prefecture. It was estimated that several hundred thousand copies had been printed. "Well," Yamazaki said, "the indiscriminate bombing has begun at last." When he showed Kazu the pamphlet he knew at once from the way she paled merely at the cover that she had seen it before. Kazu frankly described all that had happened.

"It's a shame," Yamazaki said. "A million yen means a lot to us now. Why didn't you ask my advice? You can be sure that a scoundrel like that will do all the mischief he can, regardless of whether he gets paid or not. It's obvious, of course, that the Conservative Party is behind this."

Genki Nagayama's face flashed that instant before Kazu's eyes, but she said nothing. Yamazaki continued, "The worst of it is, a lot of copies of the wretched pamphlet have found their way into the hands of suburban housewives. The aim is clear from the way it's written—to appeal to the moralistic prejudices of the *petite bourgeoise*. The suburban vote worries me a little . . . Still, on the whole it's not serious enough to bother us."

Noguchi's attitude concerning the pamphlet was truly admirable. He read it, naturally, but he never alluded with so much as a word to the scurrilous document. Kazu, badly wounded and drowning, felt that the manliness of her husband's silence was like a buoy floating silently in the dark sea.

Yamazaki was too busy now to meet either Noguchi or Kazu, and Noguchi, like an actor who forgets the director's instructions and fumbles his lines, tended in the heat of an actual campaign to forget Yamazaki's long months of guidance. Noguchi had been schooled never to lose his temper with hecklers, but he became visibly annoyed quite often. When he talked at Kichijoji, an enemy squad of twenty or more hecklers infiltrated the crowd. At one point Noguchi finally flared up at some persistent heckling and retorted, "You're probably too young to understand," at which the offenders shouted, "That's right, grandpa!" Noguchi particularly disturbed his advisers by calmly making terrible slips of the tongue in the thick of some of his discourses, without himself realizing it. For example, on three occasions the candidate of the Radical Party quite distinctly referred to "the present Imperial Constitution . . . ." Amusingly enough, Noguchi's audiences for the most part failed to notice such lapses, but his speeches, which were aridity itself, enjoyed considerable popularity among prudent, elderly persons. Yamazaki heard such reports and realized that the peculiar Japanese trust in inept talkers was by no means a thing of the past.

New incidents, large and small, were occurring at the rate of about one a minute in the different election districts. Yamazaki's voice was hoarse merely from giving instructions on the telephone about each.

"They're signs of vote-buying in A district of Suginami Ward. A lot of money seems to be floating around."

"The Investigation Squad should collect the evidence immediately and report it to the police."

"Noguchi's posters have been ripped down all over Bunkyo Ward and Tobita's pasted on top."

"Right. Paste others over them. I'll get new posters to you at once."

"Last night dirty posters were put up in the Santama district from A Street to B Street. There's about 3,000 of them, and they show a skeleton and a fat woman. They seem to be a take-off on Mr. and Mrs. Noguchi."

"Report it to the police immediately."

Yamazaki had not the least faith in the police appointed by the Conservative Party, but the young members of the Radical Party had never made daily trips to the police so joyfully. The police were obliged to thank those who informed them of violations; indeed, it seemed at this stage as if the Radical Party had become the police's favorite customer.

It had lately become a part of Noguchi's daily routine to gargle protractedly with a boric acid solution before setting out in the morning and before going to bed at night in order to soothe this throat, which grew sorer every day. At night he took a hot bath and had a massage. Only after the masseur left did Noguchi at last relax. He would sit on the bed in his pajamas, a towel under his neck, and Kazu would hold up a brass basin to catch his gargling. This somber ritual bore little resemblance to their busy activities of the day, but as Kazu lifted up the basin she felt real pleasure to think that the day had at last come to an end.

Kazu, disliking the Western-style mosquito netting which clings to the bed, had put up instead a room-sized white linen mosquito net, but even so there was not enough breeze to stir it. The glass doors facing the garden had been left open. The light from the bedside lamp permeated the motionless mosquito net, setting in relief the stiff folds in the white linen, and suggesting to Kazu that she was in some strict convent. Kazu knelt in her nightgown on the tatami and held the basin high.

She sometimes heard, at respites in Noguchi's prolonged gargling noises, the dinning of the night locusts tangled in the garden treetops. Their cries seemed to thread the night stillness with a sharp needle, but the short final notes were always twisted and sucked into the stillness. The nights in this neighborhood were astonishingly quiet. Sometimes a car would stop in the distance and drunken cries could be heard, only to disappear with the whine of the departing car.

Kazu enjoyed her posture at such times. Her body was no less tired than her husband's, but she forgot her fatigue when she pictured herself waiting on her husband in the attitude of a priestess at a shrine. This was the posture of service and self-sacrifice openly offered, and it did not matter if some spume from her husband's gargling fell on her face.

Kazu's back also ached, but she refused to be massaged

in her husband's presence. Her vocal cords, fortunately, were strong, and her voice never became hoarse, no matter how many speeches she made.

When she looked up, there would be Noguchi in his pajamas, a glass in his right hand, his left hand pushed into the quilt behind him, elaborately gargling, his head thrown back. Occasionally he inclined his head from side to side, the better to circulate the water. The lamp caught the grayish wrinkles along his thin throat. The sound came to a boil and bubbled furiously, only to halt painfully again, a sequence repeated over and over.

Kazu was enraptured by the pathos of the scene. She felt as her eyes followed him intently that she was being assimilated into her aged husband's excessive, illogical exertions. The sound of his gargling—foamy, granular, bubbling—seemed a proof that he was definitely there, alive before her. If that were true, she too was alive, and there was place for neither boredom nor inaction in such a life.

At length the third bout of gargling ended, and Noguchi, his mouth full of water, lowered his head to the basin. He spat out the water with a desolate sound, and the basin in Kazu's hands grew somewhat heavier. Noguchi sighed. His face was a little flushed.

Noguchi then, for the first time in five days of this daily routine, offered Kazu the glass and asked, "Why don't you gargle too?"

Kazu could hardly believe her ears. There would be no reason for her throat to be sore (and therefore, no necessity to gargle) unless she had been electioneering for him. For her husband to suggest that she gargle was more than mere sympathy; it clearly implied a tacit recognition of Kazu's daily efforts. The thought struck her heart with sudden joy. Looking straight into the eyes of her unsmiling husband, she reverently accepted the glass.

The newspapers, radio, and television during the first week were unanimous in reporting a lead for Noguchi. But in the second week his strength in the suburbs began to crumble. The suburban "bedroom" of Tokyo had always been a stronghold of the Radical Party; a weakening of the party's position there now was undoubtedly due largely to the effects of the scurrilous pamphlet, but party strategy all along had been to take these districts for granted and to skimp in their campaign efforts. Kazu's indomitable nature convinced her that it was still not too late. She toured the suburban residential streets in a loudspeaker truck, stopping here and there to make speeches. The well-to-do neighborhoods were torpid, most of the residents being away at summer resorts. Upper-class sections were in any case not Radical Party strongholds, so she moved on to Setagaya, the Toyoko Line and other areas with larger numbers of working people.

The truck stopped one day under a heavy canopy of greenery at the entrance to a small park. The park contained a wading pool for children, and their splashing and shouting provided an uninterrupted background noise for the speeches. A crowd gathered immediately in the vacant lot between the entrance to the park and the railway level crossing, obviously waiting for Kazu to speak. She noticed the young men in the crowd, probably delivery boys, sitting on their bicycles, one foot on the ground. Their faces, unlike those of the boys downtown and in the farming villages, had somehow sophisticated or even derisive expressions. That wasn't all—people in the audience kept whispering to one another, and gossiping every time they looked at her.

When it came time for Kazu to speak, she turned fretfully to the party worker beside her and asked, "What shall I do? They're all gossiping about me."

The middle-aged party worker knew that Kazu was haunted by the specter of the pamphlet, but to encourage her he said unconcernedly, "It's all your imagination. Give it to them, and don't pull any punches. Just look at the size of the crowd—you're a success!"

Kazu stepped forward and bowed as usual before the microphone. "I am the wife of Yuken Noguchi, the Radical Party candidate for governor." She at once caught two or three unmistakable snickers. Kazu, her face tense, spoke as in a trance. She exceeded her one-minute allowance, but the party workers today made no comment. But the more she spoke the more emptily her words scattered over the heads of her listeners.

This impression was half the product of Kazu's fears. No matter how much feeling she put into her words, one part of her mind was visualizing the figure she cut in the eyes of the crowd. She was sure people saw her in terms of the portrait in the ugly pamphlet—the poverty-stricken girl from the country who sells her body to rise in the world. She thought she detected one middle-aged man staring at her skirt. She imagined she could read his thoughts, "Humph. What's she got to do with socialism? I've heard the shameless tricks she played to make fools of men. They say that even when her body's burning up, she never forgets her ambitions. I'll bet she's cold somewhere. I wonder where it is. Do you suppose she's got a cold backside?"

A couple of groups of schoolgirls were looking at Kazu with wide-open eyes, as if they saw a monster.

Even while she was speaking, Kazu's cheeks burned with shame. She fancied she could hear words like "bedroom," "secret affair," "gold-digger," "risqué," "over-sexed" . . . The corrupt jewels that had studded the pamphlet seemed to glitter now in the crowd's gossip. The phrases from Kazu's lips—"reform of the prefectural administration," "positive policies to combat unemployment," and the like—plummeted to the ground like swarms of winged ants which have lost the strength of their wings, but the words visible on the lips of the crowd dripped like red meat in the sunshine. Old people out for a walk and leaning on their sticks, smugly respectable housewives, little girls in bare-shouldered bathing suits, delivery boys—all were gnawing on bits of Kazu's flesh, and looked at her with heavy, sated eyes.

The truck was parked in the shade, but it was extremely hot nevertheless. Kazu went on talking. She did not wipe her face with her customary ice-filled handkerchief, but let the cold sweat bathe her whole body. She could feel the eyes of the audience peeling off one layer after another of her kimonos, to leave her naked. Eyes burrowed in from the neckline, ate their way to her breasts, reached all the way to her abdomen. Invisible claws, having soaked in the sweat of her body, seemed to be ripping everything away.

This unspeakable torture gradually induced in Kazu as she stood alone on the loudspeaker truck the martyr's intoxication. A bell began to ring at the level crossing, black and white crossbars descended from the dazzling blue sky, and a long train bound for the outer suburbs rocked by with a rumbling noise. Faces at every window formed a chain of countless eyes all staring curiously toward her.

Finalyl Kazu, like a woman being burnt at the stake, lifted her eyes to the sky. Heavy cumulus clouds coiled over the low roofs. The clouds brimmed with light, and stretched grandly to the apex of the sky.

The speech ended. The truck bore Kazu, all but unconscious, to the next destination.

As it happened, the elections for ward councilors were beginning at this time. The Conservative party could consequently legally use a total of three thousand loudspeakers now, one for each candidate. Disposed at every major street corner in Tokyo, they sent out a constant barrage of attacks on Noguchi. The Radical Party barely managed to run four hundred candidates in the ward council elections, and therefore had no more than that number of loudspeakers.

Together with this development, huge sums of money started to pour into the treasury of the Conservative Party. The floodgates were open now, and the money gushed out everywhere. Kazu's funds, on the other hand, were rapidly running out, and party money-raising schemes had reached an impasse. By the eighth of August it was apparent that everything was collapsing with a roar. Not a single newspaper still predicted a victory for Noguchi.

August 9, the day before the election, was a gloomy day, a throwback to the rainy season. Rain had been falling since early morning, and it was extremely humid.

Yamazaki, as a last resort, had spent all night going through the classified telephone directory, and had compiled a list of fifty thousand names. He decided to send a telegram in the Committee Chairman's name: NOGUCHI IN TROUBLE REQUEST YOUR SUPPORT. On the morning of the ninth he took the list to the Communication Workers Union with the request that they concentrate on these telegrams and not accept any others sent in bulk. The chairman of the union gladly consented.

By the afternoon of the ninth, however, the Conservative Party had got wind of the scheme, and decided to send out opposing telegrams. These were refused at the Central Post Office. Tobita's faction immediately stirred the Minister of Postal Service into action. He issued what was in effect an administrative order, and in the course of the evening 100,000 telegrams—twice as many as the Radical Party sent—were dispatched by the Conservative Party.

That afternoon at four o'clock a telephone call came for Yamazaki, who was standing by at Noguchi's house. The place was jammed with newspaper reporters and radio and television men, and Yamazaki had to push his way through the mob to get to the telephone.

The voice at campaign headquarters was excited. "Something terrible's happened. We've just had calls from six different parts of town. Thousands of leaflets are being scattered at this minute in all six places. Some say, 'Yuken Noguchi Gravely Ill,' and some say, 'Yuken Noguchi Dying.' Newspaper boys are going through the streets shouting, 'Extra!' and distributing papers free."

Yamazaki relayed to the newspapermen present this extraordinary development. Kazu, who had been listening behind the reporters, rushed off to her room with a shriek. Yamazaki hurriedly followed. He found her lying on the floor and weeping. The room was in semi-darkness because of the rain, and the sight unspeakably gloomy.

Yamazaki stroked Kazu's back, comforting her. She suddenly straightened herself, and with an expresson broken by tears and anger, clutched the lapels of Yamazaki's suit and shook him. "You must catch whoever's responsible. You must catch them at once. Such a dirty thing to do! Such a dirty trick to try at the last minute! If this means we get beaten in the election, I'll die, and that's for sure. I've lost everything I had. And if we get beaten because of this—I'll kill whoever did it. Hurry, go out, catch them—hurry!"

Even as Kazu's voice repeated again and again the word "Hurry!" it gradually lost its strength, and soon she lay prostrate on the floor, no longer making a sound. Yamazaki left her in the care of a competent maid and, forcing his way through the hubbub in the hall, returned to his post at the telephone.

About nine that night, when everything had calmed down, the television and radio people made electrical transcriptions and films for use the following day. They were recording in advance the impressions of the new governor and his wife in the event Noguchi was elected.

There was a chilling air of unreality about such strange, childish play-acting. Noguchi answered questions unemotionally and in painstaking, colorless tones related his future aspirations for the prefectural government. The aridity of his delivery had never been heard to better advantage.

"And how about the wife of the governor?" brightly asked the announcer, and at that moment, with a perfect sense of timing, Kazu swept into the drawing room. She had changed into a splendid formal kimono. Her face was lightly powdered, and she was smiling and self-possessed—faultless, in short.

Kazu saw the newsmen to the door, then standing shoulder to shoulder with Yamazaki, said the first defeatist words he had heard issue from her mouth. "You know, Mr. Yamazaki, after all we've gone through, I somehow feel we're going to lose . . . I wonder if I ought to say such things?"

Yamazaki turned to her, but had nothing to say. But suddenly, not waiting for his reply, Kazu's face shone in the sultry darkness of the hall, as if illuminated by some inner light, and she said in a voice that sounded as if she were half dreaming, "But everything's going to be all right, isn't it? I'm sure we'll win."

CHAPTER XV

ELECTION DAY

After the rain of the preceding day, the fifteenth of August dawned perfectly clear—ideal weather for voting. Kazu arose early and made a flower arrangement in the bay window of the drawing room. She chose five water lilies of different heights and placed them in a cool-looking basin of water. Even the exertion of arranging the flowers made her perspire.

The limpid clarity of the water under the completed flower arrangement pleased Kazu. The sunrise colors of the hard, sculptural flowers floated on the surface, and the glossy, reddish-purple undersides of the leaves reflected lovely shadows in the water. Kazu felt, as she scrutinized her flower arrangement, as if she were practicing some kind of divination. She wondered if she could not find a clue to her fate in the orderly disposition of these flowers.

Kazu had thrown all her money and energies into the campaign. She had done all that human strength was capable of, and she had patiently endured every humiliation and hardship. Everyone knew that Kazu had fought well. Never before in her life had her passionate spirit been poured out so continuously and so effectively. Day after day her unique support had been her absurd conviction that once she put her mind to something she would certainly bring it to fruition. This conviction of hers normally hovered vaguely in mid-air, but during the past few months it had been planted firmly on earth, and she could no longer live without it.

Kazu attentively examined the water lilies. The water

seemed to be a symbol of the countless people who would go today to the polling places in each district. The blossoming water lilies were Noguchi himself. The water under the flowers soaked the reflections in its depths, and bubbles rose as it stirred round each tiny spike of the flower-holder. The water's only function, she thought, was to crave the favor of the lily blossoms and reflect them.

Just then a bird's shadow darted across the open bay window, and a withered leaf was flicked from a small branch reaching almost to the window. It glided sled-like through the air to drop into the basin. The water was hardly ruffled, but the shrunken yellow-brown leaf floated conspicuously on its surface. It looked ugly, like a curled-up insect.

If Kazu had not been practicing her incautious divination, she would have removed the withered leaf without giving it a second thought, but now its ominous appearance so upset her that she bitterly regretted her folly in having started this fortunetelling.

She dropped into an armchair and sat there a while, toying with a fan. A television set stood directly before her. The bluish viewing screen would soon no doubt be displaying the election returns as they came in, but now it was still a blank. The morning sunlight slanted across its surface.

Kazu took her morning bath after Noguchi, carefully made up her face, then changed to a formal kimono ordered some time previously for this occasion. After days of campaigning during which she had taken no trouble with her appearance—sometimes deliberately dressing badly—her holiday finery today braced her body. The kimono was a silvery gray gauzy silk dyed to represent a cormorant fishing scene. The cormorants were lacquer-black, and the torch flames blazed scarlet. The obi, of brocaded silk, had an embroidered design of a waning moon amid thin clouds, worked in silver thread on a pale blue background. A diamond sash clip graced her outfit.

Kazu realized that such an ornate costume was likely to annoy Noguchi, but she was determined to be dressed to her own satisfaction when she went to the polling place. In any case, now that the sweat and dust of the campaign were behind her, Kazu needed to assuage her feelings by indulging herself today, while things were still unsettled, in some luxury after her heart.

She went to the drawing room to help Noguchi with his dressing. The sight of him standing there filled Kazu's heart with joy. Noguchi was already dressed, and had himself chosen, from among the suits carefully pressed at Kazu's command, the new one he first wore on the day when he announced his intention of standing for office.

Noguchi, as usual, did not vouchsafe her even the flicker of a smile, but this thoughtfulness and his avoidance of any reference to her costume touched her deeply. In the car on the way to the polling place, they sat side-by-side in silence. Kazu looked out the window at the row of shops exposed to the merciless morning sunlight. Now that she had had such an unforgettable experience, she felt that it did not matter any more if they lost.

This, probably, was the moment of greatest intimacy between a husband and wife with such unyielding personalities. Kazu's euphoria was maintained intact until she followed her husband, through the popping flashbulbs and arc-lamps of the newspapers and newsreel cameramen, into the polling place in an elementary school, and cast her ballot in the box.

The counting of the ballots began the following day. Election forecasts printed in the three major morning newspapers showed a remarkably even distribution of opinion. One political expert predicted the victory of Tobita, another foresaw victory for Noguchi, and a third, without mentioning which side would win, predicted that it would undoubtedly be a photo finish with only a nose-length between the two men. Kazu's state of frantic excitement had started that morning. A premonition of victory agitated her, and with it the conviction that if they didn't win the world would crumble to pieces. The counting of ballots began at eight in the morning, at eleven the first bulletin was issued. Husband and wife sat before the television set in the living room. The first to report were the Santama region and the outlying metropolitan districts.

Kazu, unable to contain her palpitations, murmured as if intoning a magic spell, "It's Santama, Santama!" She suddenly recalled the string of paper lanterns on the night of the Folk Song Festival, the blackness of the surrounding mountains when the lanterns were lit, and the enthusiastic applause echoing against the mountainsides. The sunburned faces of the farm wives, their little eyes filled with curiosity, and their friendly gold-toothed smiles all came back ... She dug her fingernails into the armrests of her chair. The suspense made her feel suddenly hot and cold by turns. Finally she could keep silent no longer.

"That's a lucky sign," she cried, "Santama will be first to report. That's one place we surely won."

Noguchi did not answer.

The news bulletin flashed on the television screen, and the voice of the announcer echoed as he read:

| Yuken Noguchi | 257,802 |
| Gen Tobita | 277,081 |

The color drained from Kazu's face, but her desperate resolve not to lose hope became like a sheet of iron wrapped around her heart.

By two o'clock that afternoon the election of Gen Tobita was assured. Tobita's votes exceeded 1,600,000, and he led by a margin of close to 200,000 votes. The Conservative Party was victorious in the Osaka elections too. The radio commentators declared, "The Conservative forces have succeeded in maintaining their strategic hold on the two great cities."

Kazu wondered how she managed to keep calm in face of this travesty of justice. The enemy's victory was achieved entirely thanks to sinister machinations and money. She remembered the day, not long before the election, when the Radical Party's money started to run out, and a tremendous flood of money had poured into the Conservative Party coffers. The money swirled through the streets with manic frenzy to capture the spiritually depraved and wretched poor. The money shone like a sun through the clouds, an evil, baleful sun. And while it winked in the sky, plants with poisonous leaves wide-spread grew thick, and rank grasses, cropping out in every direction, stretched sinister feelers from here and there in the city toward the clear summer sky.

Kazu listened without shedding a tear when her husband announced that they woud go pay their respects to Radical Party headquarters.

That day Soichi Yamazaki kept missing Mr. and Mrs. Noguchi. They had already left when he visited headquarters.

A numbing sense of defeat gradually sank into Yamazaki's flesh as he busily wound up affairs at campaign headquarters. The loss of the election, to be sure, was not entirely unexpected; he himself, at least on the day before election, had in his heart clearly foreseen it. But there is always the lucky chance in ten thousand, and the characteristically unpredictable floating vote in the big cities sometimes shifts in unexpected directions. The professional's resignation had warred again and again with an irrational trusting to luck, but now a loathesome, desolate fog blanketed his mind.

The disillusion which the radical forces have always experienced in Japan had been familiar to Yamazaki since the outset of his career. Indeed, one might say that Yamazaki always wagered that he would be disillusioned; it was as if he kept up a constant bet with his youthful hopes. Yamazaki ranked as a genuine veteran in election campaigns, and he was absolutely indomitable, but a kind of masochistic fervor lodged within him. Corruption in an election or the victory of moneyed power did not in the least surprise him; they seemed as natural as stones and horse dung along a road.

As a matter of fact, it would be correct to say that the

coolness of Yamazaki's mind occasoned his love for the furnace called elections into which everything from the most valuable timber down to the filthiest scrap of paper is indiscriminately thrown. He liked the violent swings of emotions induced by self-interest among those clustering around the periphery of politics. He liked the unpredictable forces which could carry men willy-nilly to exaggerated outbursts of feelings. The incandescent heat of an election was genuine, and he liked that heat found in politics and nowhere else, whatever the tricks concealed in the background.

He enriched the empty storehouse of his mind with such pleasures, and filled the void within him with the excited emotions of many people sharing the same disaster. He enjoyed the feeling that in the end his own emotions were tinged the same hue as theirs.

To put the matter bluntly, there was something rather studied about Yamazaki's mental processes once defeat was certain and he felt heavy fog engulfing him. This epicure of disillusion was a trifle fond of pathetic scenes and sensations of defeat.

That evening, in the taxi going to Noguchi's house, Yamazaki was considering the role he would have to play, the warmhearted friend. This was the only unfinished business—he could do nothing else.

As soon as he entered the gate Yamazaki felt with his whole body the agitation in a household which has been struck by misfortune. A row of cars from the newspapers was parked before the gate, and a throng of visitors came and went, but the signs of suppressed feelings recalled the facial expressions of people paying a condolence call. Once they stepped a few yards outside the gate, they no doubt would all feel a weight lift from their shoulders, and laugh as though restored to life.

A crowd which overflowed into the hall jammed the house. Yamazaki took a look into the reception room and saw Noguchi sitting on a chair in the back of the room, surrounded by a crowd of reporters. A sound of muffled sobbing, increasing in volume, reached him from down the hall. He turned and saw Kazu exchanging downcast greetings and consoling embraces with the delegates from various groups. She was weeping.

Someone called Kazu and, hastily drying her tears, she went to the reception room, only to burst into tears again the moment she emerged. Once more she was called back to the reception room. She no longer had enough powder left in her compact to restore her face. Yamazaki put his arm around her and guided her to Noguchi's study. "Please rest here a while, Mrs. Noguchi," he said. Kazu slumped down on the carpet. Propping herself with one hand, she slowly stroked her throat with the other. She looked fixedly up at Yamazaki, the tears flowing from her wide-open eyes, like water leaking through a cracked vase.

After ten, the last reporters departed and a genuine silence descended on the house. Yamazaki, brought face-to-face with this silence, realized for the first time that this silence itself was what he and the Noguchi household had loathed and dreaded.

The smell of mosquito-repellent strengthened the wake-like atmosphere. Only the inner circle of Noguchi's associates still remained. They sat around Mr. and Mrs. Noguchi, and scarcely saying a word, drank the beer served with light refreshments. One by one they inconspicuously withdrew. Yamazaki, who had stayed to the last, was about to leave when Noguchi detained him. By then it was after eleven.

The couple led Yamazaki into Kazu's small sitting room. Noguchi spoke, "Thank you for all your trouble . . . I think I'll change to Japanese clothes." His words did not seem especially addressed to either Kazu or Yamazaki. Out of force of habit, he started to clap his hands for the maid, but Kazu stopped him. She took from the clothes basket a kimono which she had laid out for him, and helped him to change. Noguchi, accepting his sash from his wife's hands, remarked, "It's been an ordeal for you too, hasn't it? You must take it easy now."

Noguchi was weeping, his back to the others. This was the first Yamazaki had seen of his tears. Yamazaki touched his hands to the tatami in a deep bow. "I should have done better. I don't know how to apologize."

One glimpse of Noguchi's tears and Kazu was unable to restrain her sobs any longer. She threw herself down in convulsive weeping.

It was not clear to Yamazaki what had induced the couple deliberately to request his presence at this scene. He could not suppose that they needed an outside witness for their mutual revelations of heartfelt emotion. The simplest explanation was probably that the Noguchis both considered Yamazaki the closest of their intimates. Probably too, having lost all public occasion to demonstrate their great trust in him and their appreciation for all his efforts, they were left now with only this extremely private occasion. Or possibly their degree of confidence and expectation in Yamazaki had achieved something like perfect balance, and without saying so in words, they both depended on him to spare them some of the terrible silence which husband and wife should have faced alone.

Noguchi, relaxed in his Japanese clothes, addressed his wife in words overflowing with an unmistakably oriental theatricality. No one could be less theatrical than Noguchi. This was true particularly of his public life, but when, as now, it came to revealing his private, domestic emotions, ancient, heroic sentiments seemed to show themselves within him. These, one might suppose, were his deepest emotions, his true feelings stripped of all outer trappings, but actually he was possessed by the old-fashioned rhetoric of Chinese poetry. His next remarks inevitably suggested to Yamazaki, sitting beside him, T'ao Yüan-ming's *Return Home* or the lines from Po Chü-i's *Forty-five:*

Perhaps I shall build next spring
A grass hut at the foot of Mount Lu.

Noguchi's words were in fact more prosaic. He turned to Kazu, and avoiding her eyes, said in a stiff, awkward voice, "I'm giving up politics. I'll never get involved again. I had all kinds of ideals, but they don't mean anything now that I've lost. I've made you suffer too. Yes, I've really made you suffer, but from now on we'll live modestly on my pension in some quiet corner, an old man and an old woman."

Kazu, still lying on the floor, bowed her head in assent and answered meekly, "Yes." Yamazaki felt something strange about the feeling of heavy immobility in her figure. Kazu's violent emotional reactions always had an ominous tinge. Her vitality, which did not know how to be satisfied with attaining one objective, leaped ever onward; her grief might trigger unexpected elation, and her elation in turn become the portent of despair. Kazu's appearance as she crouched on the floor, radiated unquestionable grief, and the back of her obi, racked by her sobbing, confirmed this impression with its gentle embroidered design of bellflowers, but Yamazaki could detect in Kazu's body, apparently acquiescing meekly, a dark violence which had been forcibly suppressed.

When Yamazaki at last got up to leave, Noguchi politely thanked him and apologized for being too tired to see him to the door. Kazu, wiping away her tears, accompanied Yamazaki.

They turned the corner of the hall and were now opposite the front door. Kazu tugged Yamazaki's sleeve to make him stop. Her eyes, which had been heavy with grief the moment before, were shining animatedly in the dim hallway light. The stains left by her tears, hastily wiped away without regard to her appearance, criss-crossed with the shadows under her eyes and nose cast by the hallway lamp and the streaks of her face powder, to mark her face weirdly with an actor's make-up. Her expression had not changed, but her teeth flashing between her slightly parted lips and her glittering eyes made her look like some creature of the cat family stalking its prey. Her voice, which she kept low, had a domineering ring. "Damnation! We lost the election to Saeki and Nagayama's money and their lies. And that worm Tobita—I could kill him. I'd like to kill them all! Yamazaki—isn't there some way we can still drag Tobita down from his perch? Haven't you something on him? If violations of the law are what you need, there were certainly plenty of them! Haven't we some way of settling that Tobita's hash? I'm sure you can manage it, if anybody can . . . It's your duty!"

CHAPTER XVI

ORCHIDS, ORANGES, BEDROOM

Noguchi, like most men of few words, was accustomed to attach great importance to his least utterance. This was especially true of any promise involving himself, but he did not doubt, for that matter, that other people would carry through any command he imposed. It was only to be expected that anything that he thought desirable and pronounced so should come to pass. Therefore, once he had announced on the night of the defeat that henceforth he and Kazu would lead the humble existence of an elderly couple, trying to make ends meet on a pension, Noguchi assumed that Kazu was entirely resolved to obey him.

Kazu had definitely said, "Yes," that night, but during the busy days that followed, while clearing up the unfinished business left in the wake of the defeat and making thank-you calls, she became aware of the indescribable heaviness and darkness implicit in that one word "Yes." It was a sign she had consented to enter the same tomb, Kazu's hope all along. But the word was also a declaration of consent to travel together the moss-covered path that led directly to the grave.

There were various other matters to distract her. The election for the House of Counselors got underway, and speeches in support of the candidates were requested of both Noguchi and Kazu. The pleasure of helping others put them in a generous, cheerful mood, and produced a new note of humor in Noguchi's addresses and of relaxation in Kazu's. They were both more effective than when speaking in their own behalf. At dinner Kazu and

Noguchi would exchange boasts about the reactions of that day's audiences, though this had never happened during Noguchi's election campaign.

Noguchi liked to think that, having lost all he had to lose both materially and socially, he had found instead a quiet happiness. This was an excessively simple, poetic attitude, natural at Noguchi's age, but not especially natural at Kazu's. Noguchi moreover at times exaggerated this mental attitude. One day, on his way back from Radical Party headquarters he bought a potted dendrobium.

Kazu met him at the door. "Goodness—you've carried the plant yourself!" she exclaimed. "If the florist wouldn't deliver it, all you had to do was to telephone, and I'd have sent the maid to fetch it."

A tone less of concern than of annoyance was apparent in her words. She hardly looked to see what kind of flower it was. Noguchi abruptly lost his good humor. Kazu recognized the plant only after taking the pot in her hands. This was the flower Noguchi had identified for her when they lunched together at the Seiyoken Restaurant long ago.

But this discovery bothered Kazu somewhat. The thoughtfulness Noguchi displayed in wearing on election day the suit Kazu had ordered for him deeply moved her, but the orchid failed to move her in the same way. She sensed that his dried-up old hands were playing a kind of trickery intended to win her over, that it was an artifice to force a connection between orchids brushed with rouge, the faded pressed flowers in her memory, and the fresh flower of the same species before her eyes. Such coquetry on the part of a self-satisfied old man seemed an attempt to make a facile coupling of old recollections with the future, to mingle indiscriminately the frost-bitten orchids in her memory with the living orchid, and in the melancholy wreath he had thus painstakingly woven, to make Kazu his prisoner.

Kazu's defenses were aroused, but for several hours she acted as if she had noticed nothing. In their bedroom, however, she did not forget to ask, "What did you call that flower? You told me its name in the Seiyoken."

When his usual spell of coughing before going to sleep had subsided, Noguchi turned over in bed with an exaggerated rustle of his cambric summer quilt and, with the back of his white-haired head turned toward Kazu, he weariedly answered, "Dendrobium."

September came.

Kazu telephoned Yamazaki and arranged a meeting downtown, their first since the election. They agreed on the Sembikiya Fruit Parlor on the Ginza.

Kazu, dressed in a fine-patterned silk gauze, threaded her way alone through the Ginza crowds. Tanned young people, just returned from summer resorts, strolled in groups through the street. Kazu remembered the unaccountable excitement she had felt when she looked down on the inhabitants of the Ginza from the window on the fifth floor. But now the crowds were merely crowds and unrelated to Kazu. Nobody recognized her, in spite of all her speeches in every part of Tokyo. "These are the people who were off at summer resorts while we were sweating out the election," she thought.

Yet despite such momentary bitterness, she could not shake off a sense of isolation between herself and the crowd, and a feeling that all her labor had been meaningless. Smartly dressed strollers were betaking themselves to their chosen destinations, wherever their fancy led them, in the hot sunlight. The crowd was utterly devoid of mutual ties.

Kazu at length came to the entrance of the fruit parlor where she was to meet Yamazaki, and admired the window display of foliage plants with shining leaves and rare tropical fruits. She became aware of a middle-aged woman in a white suit and white hat staring at her. Kazu in turn took a good look at the woman's face. She remembered the thin-penciled eyebrows. It was Mrs. Tamaki.

Mrs. Tamaki apologized for the long lapse in her correspondence, then immediately added, "I'll never forget all the trouble I caused you at the time."

The words sounded to Kazu like an expression of deep-seated resentment. The two women stood before a bin of Sunkist oranges, and the bereaved Mrs. Tamaki, chatting all the while, was carefully removing one by one the magenta wrappers printed with thin English lettering and examining the skins of the fruit she was to buy.

"Did you go away for the summer?" she asked.

"No," Kazu answered, rather indignant.

"I only got back from Karuizawa the day before yesterday. Tokyo is still so hot."

"Yes, I don't think the summer'll ever end."

Only then did Mrs. Tamaki become aware of the meaning of the irritation in Kazu's tone. "But I returned to Tokyo, for the election, of course. Naturally I voted for Mr. Noguchi. It was a shame. I couldn't have been sorrier if it happened to myself."

"I'm most grateful for your saying so." Kazu thanked Mrs. Tamaki for her obvious lie.

Mrs. Tamaki, after much deliberation, selected three oranges. "Even oranges have become expensive these days. And just think, in America they practically give them away!" Mrs. Tamaki, as part of her brave display of inverse snobbery, deliberately ordered the salesgirl to wrap just three oranges. Kazu glanced inside the deserted parlor, wondering what was keeping Yamakazi, but the only activity was the electric fans turning on a number of empty tables.

"My husband liked oranges," Mrs. Tamaki went on. "Sometimes I offer them at the family altar. That's why I bought them today . . . You know, it suddenly occurred to me that my husband, without realizing it, of course, played the part of cupid for you and Mr. Noguchi."

"In that case, I suppose I'll have to offer him some oranges myself."

"I didn't mean it in that way."

Kazu did not herself understand why she was behaving so rudely. On a sudden impulse she motioned to the salesgirl with the sandalwood fan she had been using, and ordered her to make up a gift box of two dozen oranges.

Mrs. Tamaki turned a little pale, and glared with twitching eyes at Kazu's face, dabbing all the while with a folded lace handkerchief at the perspiration on her cheeks.

The salesgirl arranged the two dozen oranges in a large box, and decorated it with pretty wrapping paper and a pink ribbon. During this time not a word was exchanged between the two women. Kazu, gently waving her fan, sniffed the heavy fragrance of the fruit, which overwhelmed the delicate scent of her sandalwood fan, and savored the full bracing pleasure of this silence. Kazu utterly detested the woman before her. Her hatred was immoderate, and the pleasure of this silence afforded her the best cure she had for depression in a long time.

Mrs. Tamaki looked like a secret agent brought to bay. Kazu understood precisely the calculations which were going through her mind, and this gave her additional pleasure. Mrs. Tamaki was thinking that if it was Kazu's intention when the wrapping was completed to offer the gift to someone else, she would be humiliated by her own groundless fears, but if, on the other hand, Kazu intended to offer the oranges to the memory of Ambassador Tamaki, Mrs. Tamaki would be even more humiliated. She was too agitated to look directly as the salesgirl busily executed an exceptionally fancy bow with the ribbon.

Finally the widow's eyes met Kazu's squarely. "Upstart!" Mrs. Tamaki's eyes were saying. "Liar!" Kazu's eyes said. She was sure that once Mrs. Tamaki got home she would nibble voluptuously on the three imported oranges . . .

"Well, I'm sure I'll be seeing you soon. Oh, I'll have the oranges delivered. I don't want to burden you with them now. Please offer them to the departed one." Kazu pointed with her fan at the box of oranges, wrapped at last.

"Really! What does this mean? How perfectly horrid! Really!"

Mrs. Tamaki, still muttering incoherently, fled into the street filled with glaring afternoon sunlight, her small paper parcel under her arm. The sharply pointed heels of her white shoes lingered in Kazu's eyes as she watched the retreating figure, and rendered her satisfaction all the more delicious. She thought that Mrs. Tamaki looked like a white fox escaping.

Yamazaki entered the shop just after Mrs. Tamaki left. He still retained his air of harassment from the campaign.

"You're late, aren't you?" Kazu said in accents of heartfelt joy as they walked toward the back of the parlor.

They settled themselves in chairs and ordered cold drinks. The shopgirl came to ask where the oranges should be delivered. Kazu, not wishing to mention Tamaki's name before Yamazaki, asked the girl to bring the telephone directory. She ran her finger down the page until she came to Mrs. Tamaki's address.

"I thought that such extravagant presents were strictly forbidden now," commented Yamazaki.

"Please don't say that. I need a change from too much shouting of 'Please give me your support!' all the time."

Yamazaki was unable to grasp her meaning. He covered the uncertain look on his face with the hot towel brought by the waitress.

Kazu asked casually, "What's ever happened to the Setsugoan?"

"It's quite a story."

"It has to be broken up into lots, I suppose."

"Yes, I don't see any other way. There's a difference of forty or fifty million yen involved ... I've talked with a lot of real estate agents, and they all come to the same conclusion. If you sell the property as it is, the most you can hope for is one hundred million, and you won't find a buyer at a moment's notice. A garden that size and an imposing building ..."

"Does the price include the furnishings?"

"Of course. But if you offer the property in lots of four hundred or eight hundred square yards, you'll have no trouble raising 140 or 150 millions. It's a good location."

"Then it's your conclusion, I take it, that I should divide?"

"It's a pity, but there's no choice."

"I'm too stunned to call it pity or anything else."

"Yes, I know, the garden and the building are in the National Treasure class. But still," Yamazaki stole a glance at Kazu's face, "I don't suppose you could reopen it."

"No, that's out of the question. I've taken out three mortgages on the property to the tune of eighty-five million yen, and there's a mortgage of seven million yen on the movables . . . It's not a sum of money you can pay back overnight, even if the restaurant does pretty well. It's only been four months and a little more since I shut the place, but it doesn't take people long to forget these days. There's one other thing I haven't told you, but while I was away three million yen of the restaurant's money were embezzled. That's what you call rubbing salt into a wound, isn't it? . . . In any case, reopening the restaurant is impossible. I've solemnly promised my husband to sell the Setsugoan, and after asking your help with the negotiations, I really can't back out now."

Yamazaki had no way to refute this admirable statement of the situation. "What can I do for you today?" he asked, after draining the chilled grape juice in one gulp.

"Nothing special. I wanted to ask you about dividing the Setsugoan, and I thought I might invite you to go with me to the movies for a little distraction."

"Did you leave Mr. Noguchi alone in the house?"

"No. Today he went to attend a high school class reunion or something of the sort. He was afraid that if he didn't show up people would say it was because he was ashamed to have lost the election. I got permission to go out by telling him that an old friend was giving a recital. I took the precaution of sending a present to the dressing room, just to make sure."

"Those oranges a little while ago?" Yamazaki had not heard their destination.

"Yes, that's right."

"You think of everything, don't you, Mrs. Noguchi?"

They exchanged glances and laughed. Then they returned to a more businesslike matter—Noguchi's determination last month, after much pondering, to wind up his affairs. He had decided to sell his house and all the furnishings, pay his debts, then move to a small rented house already selected in a remote part of the suburbs. Noguchi's tangible personal property was by no means negligible, and together with the house and land was likely to fetch fifteen or sixteen million yen. The auction of the property would be held on the deserted premises of the Setsugoan. Noguchi's collection of paintings, antiques, and rare European books had already been carted off to the Setsugoan.

"The auction's the day after tomorrow, isn't it?" Yamazaki asked.

"Yes. I only hope it doesn't rain."

"What difference does it make?"

"But they'll have to use the garden, won't they? You should know, Mr. Yamazaki."

They sent for an evening paper and tried to pick a movie worth seeing. It would have to be something light and amusing since their purpose was to be diverted. The trouble was that Kazu disliked comedies.

Kazu leaned her head over the newspaper spread before them, all but brushing her cheek against Yamazaki's. He watched with oppressive feelings her ringed fingers, white and delicate, travel down the columns of print. "What am I to her?" he asked himself. Only when she was with a man she did not love could Kazu behave like a natural lover, an easy-going mistress; she was simple, capricious and even showed a touch of rusticity. But in the presence of man she loved, Kazu's "naturalness" disappeared. Yamazaki was unquestionably seeing a Kazu completely unknown to Noguchi. But Yamazaki had no reason to feel especially grateful for this privilege.

Their efforts to select a suitable film ended by thoroughly wearying them. Kazu said, "I don't feel like going to the movies any more."

"You don't have to force yourself. There's no point in looking too hard for amusement at this stage. You're busy now and there are things to distract you, but by-and-by an emptiness you can't do a thing about will come over you. An emptiness you won't even want to lift a finger against." Thus spoke the expert on elections.

The auction of Noguchi's property took place at the Setsugoan two days later, beginning in the morning. Noguchi had put up every last possession for sale.

The large household objects were set out on a carpet spread over the lawn. The sunlight was remarkably intense that day, a day that suggested summer had returned. A pair of beds on the lawn caught the attention of prospective buyers. These were the twin beds in which Mr. and Mrs. Noguchi had slept until the previous night. They created a strangely pathetic, raw impression, despite the damask bedspreads now covering them. The twin beds were placed apart from the other furniture in the center of the lawn. The pale green damask shone with an unpleasantly strong luster in the glaring early autumn sunlight. The beds, however, seemed curiously in their element in the middle of the garden with its unmowed grass so high it smelled like hay, the blue sky visible at breaks in the rows of tall pines, chestnuts, and nettle trees.

One irreverent customer remarked, "That's certainly convenient. They ought to leave the beds there all the time."

As twilight approached the shadows of the branches fell on the beds, and the voices of the evening cicadas enveloped them.

CHAPTER XVII

A GRAVE
IN THE EVENING CLOUDS

Nothing so frightened Kazu as Yamazaki's prediction that an emptiness would soon steal over her against which she would not want to move a finger. When would it come? Ten days hence? Tomorrow? Or perhaps it had come already, and she merely hadn't noticed it?

The thought produced in Kazu an indescribable weariness. She had no confidence that she could endure the predicted emptiness. She had, it is true, experienced emptiness a number of times in her life, but she had a premonition that this time it would be on an incomparably vaster scale than before. She tried in various ways to picture the features of this monster, but her imagination did not extend to something she had never seen. No matter how dreadful a face it might have, she would be glad at last if it had one, for the monster might be faceless.

Her experience during the election had opened Kazu's eyes to her own nature. The self she had previously believed in only vaguely had been dissected, and many precise characteristics—how strong this part was, how weak that one was, how much patience she could show under certain circumstances, how much she leaned in a certain direction—were now clear, and she knew now that she could never again bear any form of emptiness. Full, if tragic, circumstances were preferable to a void. Kazu far preferred the north wind tearing her body to a vacuum.

During these fretful deliberations, however, gilt letters kept flashing constantly in her head, saying, "Reopen the Setsugoan." The project was hopeless, indeed impossible, and there was no way to alter this situation. Kazu was well aware of the fact. Yet this knowledge did not prevent her eyes from being drawn incessantly to the little sun shining like silver in a corner of the overcast sky. The impossibility was the source of its radiance. It glittered. It hung beautifully in the heavens. However often she averted her eyes, they would return to this brilliance, again because of its impossibility. And once her glance had traveled there, everywhere else seemed only darkness.

For days Kazu balanced in her mind the coming emptiness against the impossible reopening. She was famed for the rapidity of her decisions, but she could not make up her mind between these two exceedingly vague and formless alternatives. In such a predicament, what good would it do even to consult a reliable astrologer?

She tried to review as carefully as she could the several months of the election. The Conservative Party, she realized, had not won because of its political principles. Nor had it won because of its logic, its lofty sentiments, or the superiority of its candidate. Noguchi was indisputably a splendid man, his logic was impeccable, and he possessed noble sentiments. The Conservative Party had won entirely thanks to its money.

This was certainly a crude lesson, and it was not to be taught such a lesson that Kazu had poured her energies into the election. A belief in the omnipotence of money was not especially novel to Kazu. But when she had used her money she had at least thrown in her heart and her prayers, while her opponents' money advanced like a robot, trampling all before it. The conclusion Kazu reached was not so much regret that her money had been insufficient as regret that her heart and Noguchi's logic had been expended to no avail. It was regret that the human tears, smiles, friendly laughter, warmth of flesh—everything Kazu believed in during this campaign to which she had devoted her heart and soul—had proved futile.

This came to her almost as a physical shock, and made her lose faith in her tears and the magic of her smiles. It was a common-sense assumption of the old-fashioned society in which Kazu grew up that a woman's attractions were a powerful weapon which could conquer money and authority, but such a belief now seemed to Kazu, in the light of her experiences during the election, no more than a distant myth. This was Kazu's blunt evaluation of the election: "femininity" had been beaten by "money." It was the opposite of the clear victory of flesh when a woman abandons her indigent lover to give herself to a rich man she does not love.

Noguchi's defeat was reflected in Kazu's eyes as a natural corollary to this principle: the "man" Noguchi was beaten by "money."

Kazu felt hatred and indignation for this power which had so ruthlessly demonstrated the ineffectuality of logic, sentiments, physical attractions, and the rest, but she soon perceived also that this mental blind alley was inseparably linked to the impossibility of reopening the Setsugoan. Until the last days of the election she had kept alive within her a belief in the power of miracles to change the impossible into the possible. Now that was dead. Her confidence in a miracle at the end of the election campaign could certainly be said to have been a confidence in politics itself, but politics had not responded to this confidence, and Kazu in turn had completely lost her mystic confidence in politics.

But if such reasons were enough to make Kazu despair of politics, it meant that, like Noguchi, she thought that logic, sentiments, and personal charms constituted the whole of politics. Only these factors, after all, had been exposed as ineffectual. And, it occurred to her, if politics had given her the courage to look for a miracle when the situation around her seemed virtually hopeless, politics —regardless of the outcome—deserved all the less to be despaired over.

The result of thinking in these terms was that the meaning of politics was suddenly transfigured for Kazu.

Her efforts had proved utterly fruitless, but if she flung aside what was doomed to be futile, and relied entirely on her confidence in miracles, perhaps the impossible would become possible, and politics would again come to her aid.

Perhaps the glimmering confidence in miracles which her ideals had lit and the efforts to achieve miracles which realism had summoned forth were, in the realm of politics, the same.

The reopening of the Setsugoan might not be impossible.

In the midst of these reflections a splendid political discovery hatched in Kazu's mind: "The Conservative Party won with its money. That's why I'm faced with losing the Setsugoan. It's only fair that Conservative Party money should compensate me."

This was truly a noteworthy revelation.

Kazu, choosing a time when her husband was not at home, telephoned the residence of In Sawamura in Kamakura. Sawamura, a monumental figure in the forces of Japanese Conservatism, had served as Prime Minister any number of times. Kazu was an old acquaintance of Sawamura's common-law wife.

Kazu's heart pounded despite herself as she dialed the number. Now, for the first time (though she herself did not realize it) Kazu had approached the essence of politics—betrayal.

The Sawamura family had been for generations worshippers of the goddess Benzaiten, and in deference to this exceedingly jealous virgin goddess, In Sawamura had never married. He had taken a geisha named Umeme as his common-law wife, and to keep up appearances treated her exactly like a servant. Umeme had never once come to the fore or uttered a word in the presence of guests. She still referred to the man who was in fact her husband as "His Excellency."

Umeme answered Kazu's request for an appointment quite unaffectedly. "I'm sure that His Excellency will be glad to see you, but I'll inquire first about his convenience."

In the end, a meeting was arranged for eleven in the morning on the fifteenth of September. This appointment could not be changed.

The following day Kazu learned that Noguchi had set the fifteenth of September for the removal to the rented house in Koganei. She was dumbfounded at this extraordinarily unlucky break. She felt sure that if she asked for a postponement of the meeting Sawamura would not grant her a second one. She tried desperately to think how she could slip away on the day of the removal. It was obvious that a housewife must be present on such an occasion. The date of the removal had been determined singlehandedly by Noguchi; as usual, he saw no need to consult with his wife on the matter. It was beyond Kazu's powers to alter the date.

Once again Kazu felt the strength to make rash decision surging up within her. The day before removal, she went back to the Setsugoan, alleging that she had things to dispose of. Complaining of a severe headache, she summoned her neighborhood physician, and persuaded him to telephone the Noguchi house and state in his own words that it was advisable for her to spend the night at the Setsugoan. Early the next morning the physician was again summoned, and once again she induced him to telephone Noguchi, this time with the message, "It's quite out of the question for her to help with the moving today. She must be allowed to rest quietly until evening."

Kazu hastily got rid of the physician, then dispatched the two young maids to help with the removal, keeping with her only her confidential maid. Kazu rose from her sickbed with remarkable vigor. The maid, understanding the situation, laid out the clothes Kazu would wear. The kimono was an unlined garment of slubbed crepe dyed in shades of sepia with a design of primroses at the hems. The obi had a pattern of insects embroidered in green and silver on a white ground. Kazu, baring herself to the waist, began her toilet before a mirror in the early morning sunlight. The maid stood beside her attentively. Kazu had no need to say a word; a flicker in her eyes reflected in the mirror was enough for the maid to provide whatever was necessary. The maid sensed that the important errand of the proprietress this morning would decide their future.

Kazu's rich shoulders and breasts had lost nothing of

their beauty, despite all the summer's exertions. Her sunburned neck, however, emerging light-brown, like a faded flower, from the snow-white skin below, showed the effects of the election campaign. The sunlight striking the surface of the mirror still kept a lingering summer intensity, but Kazu's white shoulders and breasts were an icehouse. The fine-grained, saturated whiteness repelled the light, suggesting that it concealed within a cool, dark summer interior.

It was nothing short of astonishing how little indication of her age Kazu's skin gave. Her skin seemed to have slipped softly through the hard fetters of age. This pliant skin, which hid an alertness and cunning beneath its normal composure, had a smooth self-sufficiency, like milk filling a basin to the brim. Her extremely fine pores seemed to expand self-indulgently in the morning sun, giving her skin a mellower glow than ever.

"What a lovely skin you have!" the maid said. "It's enough to make even a woman want to pounce on you!"

"I have no time for compliments," Kazu answered. In her heart she permitted and accepted this praise, but her eyes were directed toward the mirror with an intensity bordering on ferocity. She daubed her skin with toilet water, had the maid apply it to the nape of her neck, then patted powder on top. She used foundation cream to shade off the excessively sharp line of demarcation of her sunburn. Kazu had never thrown herself with such concentration and strain into her beauty preparations, nor had she ever had so little time.

"The car's ready to leave whenever I want, isn't it?"

"Yes, madam."

Kazu ordered the maid to send for the chauffeur even as she began her dressing. The young chauffeur came as far as the corridor outside her room and knelt on one knee at the door. The proprietress of the Setsugoan, busy tying her undersash, gave the chauffeur a hard look. "You're not to tell anybody where we're going today—do you understand? If anybody finds out, there'll be hell to pay. No matter who asks you, you'll be sorry if you tell."

That evening Kazu returned to the Setsugoan in unusually good spirits. She had been urged to remain when she started to leave Sawamura's house, and that hard-to-please old man had taken lunch with her. Kazu described everything to her trusted maid. She took a quick bath to wash off the talcum powder. Then she changed to a conservative kimono and set off immediately for the new house in Koganei.

Noguchi made no comment. He merely inquired briefly about her condition and did not listen very carefully to her answer.

Seeing how the removal was progressing was enough to inspire Kazu with fresh thoughts about the coldness of the world. The Radical Party had sent only two clerks, and there was no sign anywhere of the young people who had flocked so enthusiastically to Noguchi during the campaign. Yamazaki was there, clumsily carrying a tea cabinet. The only other helpers were the houseboy and the maids, originally from the Setsugoan.

The house faced the Koganei Embankment, not far from the Hara-Koganei Station on the Seibu Electric Line. The paved road along the opposite bank of the waterworks canal was the Itsukaichi Highway. The road on this side was unpaved. The grass on the embankment and the hedges before the house were white with dust.

The new houses had seven rooms and a fairly large garden, but it was of cheap construction and shook every time a truck passed by. The gate posts were trees of natural growth, and the garden also boasted a willow, a cedar, and a hemp palm, among other attractions.

By the following afternoon the house was in sufficiently good order for Mr. and Mrs. Noguchi to take their first walk. They strolled for a while upstream on a path over the weed-covered embankment.

Kazu's only remembrances of living in such a countrified place went back to the distant days of her girlhood. Heavy traffic flowed over the Itsukaichi Highway, but apart from an occasional truck or bicycle they saw nothing resembling a car on this bank, and they naturally encountered no one along the path. Kazu noticed for the first time in years how hollow a dog's barking sounds in the daytime.

The path hummed with the chirpings of many kinds of insects. The huge masses of pampas grass were already in ear, and their feathery spikes, bending gracefully, shone a fresh silver. The bamboo grass and the tall weeds, dust-covered only on the side facing the road below, brought to mind some exquisite work in plaster of Paris, but the grass around the path under the avenue of cherry trees had been left to grow wild, and one could imagine the sultry grass fumes in summer. The grass grew so thick that they could not even glimpse the surface of the canal. Chestnuts and silk trees stretched their branches unhindered across the water; here and there branches from both banks interlaced, and vines twisted round them. All they could hear was the rather lighhearted sound of the water below. If they had wished to see the water they would have had to step to the edge of the grass-covered embankment and risk falling over.

The path was too narrow for them to walk abreast. Noguchi therefore went ahead. He had put up at auction even his snakewood walking stick, and he now used a crudely made stick of cherrywood to clear away the grass in his path. Kazu noticed that the hair at the back of Noguchi's head had turned completely white. His withered shoulders—perhaps this was only her imagination—had lost their dignity, and the back of his gray shirt smacked of the retired old gentleman.

Kazu, however, was aware that Noguchi was deliberately pretending. He was trying by choice to act the part of the retired old gentleman. His failure to inquire seriously into Kazu's absence of the day before, his bland good humor even during the confusion of the removal, when normally he would have flown into a rage—these and other instances were indicative of Noguchi's new posture. In the attempt to enjoy his leisure, after having lost all else, he looked for the seeds of pleasure in every manner of thing. But they were not to be found in a moment. Consequently, Noguchi's present cheerfulness had something solemn and high-principled about it, a reflection of his former code.

When, for example, they went out on this walk, Noguchi praised the clear air of the suburbs and pronounced the words, "Ah, this is really pleasant," a total of three times, each time, it is true, with a somewhat different emphasis.

Once Noguchi had fixed his mind on a definite objective, he could not rest until he had adjusted and integrated all other things accordingly. He believed that they would promote his high-principled good cheer, that everything would lend strength. Or so he dreamed. A man with political aspirations has rivals, but a man with poetical aspirations should not expect to have any . . . At present there was still disharmony. Many things remained to be adjusted. But presently everything would be purified, would progress toward harmony and be guided to the "quiet on the hilltop" of Goethe's *A Wanderer's Night-Songs*.

Kazu walked with her eyes down. She noticed fragments of green soft-drink bottles and brown beer bottles deeply imbedded in the earth along the path. Washed by the wind and the rain, they were now solidly inlaid, and seemed to have been there a very long time. Kazu spoke. "There must be a lot of merrymaking here when the cherry blossoms are in bloom."

Her words broke the spell of Noguchi's reveries. But he had an answer carefully prepared. He replied cheerfully, "No, I gather there's not much of that any more. The cherry trees around here have become pretty old, and they're not looked after properly. The blossoms are not very impressive. The loud merrymakers all congregate around the cherry blossoms in Koganei Park, I'm told. We won't be bothered by them. Yamazaki was saying so."

"I'm glad to hear that." A certain regret trailed through Kazu's words. She herself was only vaguely aware of the cause for this regret. Kazu was dreaming of the crowds.

Noguchi paused under a cherry tree and poked with his walking stick into the damp hollows of the trunk. "Look," he said, "it won't be long before this one rots to pieces." His lively gesture with the stick accentuated his old age all the more. Kazu shrank to see how his eyebrows, like worn-out brooms, cast shadows over the gentle smile in his eyes.

Noguchi's words, delivered in his rather unnaturally cheerful voice, pricked Kazu's heart one by one like transparent glass fibers. She actually felt unpleasant not to have been scolded for what she did the day before.

She had gone the previous day to In Sawamura with a subscription book for the reopening of the Setsugoan. Kazu broached this request on two levels, in her usual manner. First, she launched precipitously into a request that Sawamura use his influence to persuade the present Minister of Finance and the Minister of Trade and Industry to make special arrangements for a loan. After brief consideration, Sawamura replied that it would be difficult for him, and such highhanded policies would not in any case be to Kazu's advantage under the circumstances.

Kazu, rebuffed in the first instance, moved to her second stage. She produced the subscription book and begged him to sign. If, she said, Sawamura's name headed the list, nobody would refuse to join. Sawamura apologized with a sardonic smile for being unable, as a retired person, to offer more than a token. He ordered Umeme to prepare some Chinese ink, then wrote with a brush in a splendid hand, "Ten Thousand Yen. In Sawamura."

It was safe to assume that nobody as yet knew of this. Once the subscription list had been circulated among the various people Sawamura had suggested—Prime Minister Saeki, Genki Nagayama, and many other men in the world of finance—the secret would be discovered, of course, but for the moment it was inconceivable that Noguchi could have heard of it.

The instant Kazu secured Sawamura's signature in her book, this unexpected success had caused her heart to burst into flames. Once again her energies spread in every direction like wildfire, and she felt an incomparable joy. The one thing that had weighed on her mind since the preceding night was how to disguise her joy. Kazu finally decided to bend her body to her will, like a feline curbing its excessive energy, and while disbursing a modicum of good cheer, the proper amount to accord with her husband's new-found happiness, to do her utmost to maintain an expression of gloom. This unnatural effort, however, strained her nerves unnecessarily . . . Kazu thought that the sensitivity of her nerves accounted for her vague apprehensions over Noguchi's generosity.

But the thought that Noguchi knew nothing made his figure strolling along in his gray shirt, his walking stick held over him, seem unspeakably solitary and tragic; she felt it would be a great relief if Noguchi would only find out. Kazu was not sufficiently aware of having committed a crime to wish to punish herself. At the same time, she hoped a little for Noguchi's understanding.

"Look!" said Noguchi, again pausing and pointing his stick at the opposite bank. "Just think, in this day and age, such tea stalls still exist! It looks like something out of a play, doesn't it?"

Kazu looked and saw on the opposite bank, facing the highway, an old-fashioned combination eating place and tea stall. Below the slanting eaves was a display door with a glass panel on top. Slips of varicolored paper dangled from the glass part of the door, and a red carpet covered the lower part. The signs were inscribed in large letters: "Vegetable Stew," "Dumplings," and the like.

"How picturesque!" Kazu said with an exaggerated sigh of admiration. She started to step into the grass, which was covered with thick, heavy cobwebs, but Noguchi swiftly swept them away with the point of his stick. The cobweb threads entangled round the stick hovered lightly about it; when the slanting rays of the sun caught them, a delicate glimmering spread slowly in the air.

Kazu was unable to maintain her heavy silence any longer. She burst out with a quite unnecessary suggestion. "You know, it's a very quiet, livable house, but I think we'd do well to remodel the bathroom at least. It's a rented house, of course, but we'll be there a long time."

"I was thinking the same thing," said Noguchi satisfiedly. "It would be nice when I get back from golfing to have a pleasant bath waiting for me."

"Golfing? Yes, you told me that you used to play a long time ago, when you were abroad . . . But what will you do for clubs?"

"I've been thinking that once my life settles into a routine I'll search the secondhand shops and pick up a set—cheap ones will do. I'll start again. What gave me the idea was having the Koganei Golf Links so near. I'll invite my old friends, and once in a while some foreign friends . . ."

"That's a fine idea. Yes, I certainly hope you'll take up your golf again. It'll do you a world of good. I'd been thinking that the worst thing for your health after all that strenuous exercise this summer would be to stop everything suddenly." Kazu assented, showing an unfeigned pleasure. Her husband would have to move around a bit.

They reached the first bridge over the canal. Leaning on the iron pipe which served as a handrail on this unpretentious little bridge, they looked down through the interlacing leafy branches and caught their first glimpse of the canal. The water flowed fairly swiftly, its surface dappled by the light streaming through the chestnut leaves.

"It's like a lamé obi," said Kazu, "though that's not a fashion I particularly admire."

Noguchi added, "It's the first time I've seen water since coming here."

They soon climbed back on the embankment, their faces to the sun in the west, and continued their walk upstream.

Even as they exchanged such remarks Kazu realized that her eyes were now looking down on the scene from some great height. Far below her she could see two tiny figures, an old couple walking along the embankment. Noguchi's white hair shone, the coral beads of Kazu's

171

hairpin shone and occasionally when Noguchi brandished his stick it too gave off a little flash of light. The emotions of the old couple were transparent, filled with melancholy: they overflowed with human loneliness. No foreign element could be intruded.

But to look at things in this manner was naturally for Kazu also a means of self-defense. If she did not, her existence held a blade so sharp that it would surely wound herself and her husband; unless she could view things from a height, this touching picture of an aged couple out for their melancholy stroll would suddenly change and be transformed into a picture too ugly to bear contemplation.

Noguchi was plainly enjoying every moment of this serene walk. The signs of his pleasure were apparent in his carriage, in his eyes when from time to time he looked up at the sky, in his walk, in his way of swinging his stick. But she could detect in his enjoyment an exclusive, obstinate quality; Kazu's existence did not seem absolutely indispensable. Kazu thought as she walked behind Noguchi that she must give him the sympathy of a person who steals a glance over an artist's shoulder at the picture he is painting on canvas. Now she lacked even the qualifications to bother Noguchi. She must not disturb his thoughts.

Kazu's sympathy was extended to each instant illuminated by the afternoon sun of late autumn. She could understand that Noguchi, aware also that he would not be blessed a second time with such a well-ordered, serene state of mind, should try desperately to preserve this serenity. Kazu had no wish to destroy it now. She had no reason to deny that each successive moment—even if it was a sham—was creating a picture of a kind of happiness.

They saw how the rays of the sun, slanting into a grove of tall cryptomerias to the left of the road, caused a mysterious, golden mist to coil between the trunks of the trees. A truck passed alongside, raising an immense cloud of dust. The dust remaining drifted among the cryptomerias, and again turned a peaceful gold.

They saw too the sun sink beautifully in the sky ahead of them as they walked. The sunset clouds tinted the clumps of trees here and there in colors like those of fresh vegetables. The evening clouds glowed vividly, but amidst their flaming there was also one scrap of cloud which contained the colors of darkness. Kazu recognized in this dim gray fragment the shape of a gravestone, the gravestone of the Noguchi family.

Strangely enough, the familiar vision of this gravestone, which always stirred Kazu's heart, today failed to evoke any excitement. She thought vaguely that it would be her grave, but she watched undisturbed as the gravestone trailed distantly, indistinctly in the sky. The gravestone tumbled over, collapsed, dissolved . . . And the bright evening clouds around it suddenly turned the color of ashes.

CHAPTER XVIII

AFTER THE BANQUET

In Ocotober Noguchi received a dinner invitation from the old friends with whom he had gone to the Omizutori Ceremony in Nara. Kazu was not invited.

The usual forces gathered in a spacious room overlooking the Sumida River in a geisha establishment in Yanagibashi. No doubt the same newspaper which had paid for the trip to Nara was paying this time too. The octogenarian journalist sat in the place of honor. Noguchi, the newspaper executive, and the financial critic made up the rest of the party.

Halfway through the dinner Noguchi got up to go to the lavatory, and the old man followed him. A geisha started to lead him by the hand, but he firmly rebuffed her. He stopped Noguchi at a corner of the hallway and said, "You may already have heard about it, Noguchi, but the others decided that we had to tell you in case you didn't know. The unpleasant task fell on me, as the oldest. It's really difficult to know how to begin," the old man hesitated, "but your wife has recently been circulating among various people in the cabinet and the financial world a subscription book for the reopening of the Setsugoan. I gather that In Sawamura was the first she approached, and she seems as a result to have collected quite a lot of money. I don't suppose this comes as news to you."

"No, it's the first I've heard of it," Noguchi interrupted hurriedly.

Noguchi's distress when he returned to the party was plainly visible to the other guests. A glance at his expression and they understood that the old journalist had broken the news, and that Noguchi had suspected nothing.

Their sympathy for Noguchi was apparent from the kindness they showed him. These men were sufficiently polished to manage such a difficult and delicate expression of friendship, but their polish wounded Noguchi all the more. He excused himself. A message had been left for him that Kazu would spend that night at the Setsugoan. She had not returned to the house in Koganei.

While Noguchi was in Yanagibashi, Kazu was seeing Genki Nagayama in Akasaka.

Nagayama, when she first requested a meeting, had answered lightly, obviously well aware of everything, "I suppose it's your subscription book." Kazu suggested a meeting at his "office," but he insisted on an expensive restaurant of his choosing in Akasaka. It embarrassed Kazu to join Nagayama at this restaurant, which was run by an acquaintance, but in the end she went. She arrived punctuallly, and was then kept waiting half an hour.

While Kazu waited, the proprietress made various attempts to engage her in conversation, a torture to Kazu. The old woman had heard rumors about the reopening of the Setsugoan, and she wanted Kazu to know that she was completely on her side. She gave her encouragement as well. "It was clever of you to get Mr. Sawamura's signature. You'd never have got far without it. You've had such a hard time of it, Mrs. Noguchi, you're due to blossom out now." The proprietress eagerly offered to introduce Kazu to a fortuneteller whose predictions were amazingly accurate. It would help in the business, she said. Kazu accepted the offer without enthusiasm. She was afraid, for one thing, of an unfavorable prediction at the very outset, but more importantly, Kazu had faith now exclusively in her own unaided activity.

They heard noises emanating from the far end of the corridor. The proprietress jumped to her feet and cried out in a voice of earsplitting brightness, "We're tired of waiting! You should never keep a lady waiting!"

Nagayama's voice could be heard, indifferent as ever to the surroundings, "She's no lady. The old dame's a crony of mine."

"What a thing to say!"

Kazu, sitting formally, trembled slightly with apprehension. She sat again amidst this type of joke, this type of excessive familiarity, this type of broad-minded bad manners. However she might repudiate them, the fact was that she was sitting here. Nagayama had never once attempted to treat her as the wife of a former cabinet minister.

Kazu felt closer now to politics than when she was caught in the whirlpool of a fierce election campaign. She felt as if only now—when surrounded by such jokes, by cheerful banter, by women's laughter, by the fragrance of incense rising in the tokonoma, by this whole chain of things—did politics first register on all her five senses. Only in this atmosphere could politics show its face and work miracles.

Genki Nagayama strode into the room. He was in Japanese clothes. He greeted Kazu with genuine affability, then sat down, across the table from her.

Kazu, still sitting rigidly erect, gave the face of the ugly old man a hard look. His florid complexion indicated an unpleasant abundance of energy, and gave the impression of flesh quarreling with flesh. His eyes, set in layers of heavy wrinkles, stared out nakedly, as if the wrinkles did not exist. The perfectly white rows of a complete set of false teeth faintly clinked behind his big, thick lips.

Kazu, her eyes riveted to his face, pronounced the word, "Devil!"

"Is that all you have to say?" Nagayama asked, grinning.

"Coward! Monster! The dirtiest villain of them all, that's you. That disgusting pamphlet—*The Life of Mrs. Yuken Noguchi*—you were behind that too, don't try to deny it. You haven't a scrap of decency in you. You stink worse than a worm in a privy. You're the lowest species of human kind. You're a cesspool clogged with all the filthy things no normal human being would even think of. I can't understand how you've managed to stay alive all this time without getting yourself killed. I honestly think I could rip you into eight pieces, and still not feel satisfied."

Kazu grew more and more agitated as she spoke. She

had the feeling that her words themselves were driving her on. Her face was terribly flushed, her mouth dry, and tears flowed uncontrollably from her wrathful eyes. Sobbing hysterically, she poured out her abuse. Her hand pounded the table hard enough to smash her turquoise ring. Of course it would not matter if that ring got broken. Kazu never wore her diamond ring when she took around the subscription book.

Nagayama listened, nodding and occasionally interposing, "Is that so?" Presently, however, his eyes blurred with quite incomprehensible tears that flowed down his cheeks along the thick wrinkles. "Yes, I understand," he said in a heavy voice. "Go on. Say it all." He clenched his fists covered with reddish hairs and wiped his eyes. A thick, sweet voice, like a nurse's humoring a baby in a cradle, issued from the lips of this ugly old man. "I understand. I understand. How you must have suffered ... You must have suffered terribly."

Nagayama's hand reached gently from his side of the table to touch Kazu's heaving shoulders. Her face was hidden by the handkerchief before her eyes, but she sensed his presence, and with her shoulder repulsed his hand.

"It's all right, it's all right," Nagayama's voice sounded strained now because he had stooped over and thrust his head under the low table. His hand stretched out to the parcel wrapped in lavender crepe by Kazu's knee. Nagayama placed the parcel on his lap and undid the knots. He removed the subscription book, and slowly turned the thick pages bound in Japanese style. He wiped his eyes again and again with the back of his hand even as he turned the pages.

A little while later Kazu noticed Nagayama searching for the bell to summon the maid. Kazu, ashamed to be seen by the maid, turned her back to the door, and took the handkerchief from her face.

The maid appeared. "Bring me a writing set," Nagayama commanded. The maid came back with the set and began to rub the ink stick on the stone. Kazu felt compelled to hide her tears for appearances' sake. She opened her compact and tidied her face. The maid, frightened by the strange silence and tears of the two guests, disappeared as soon as she had finished preparing the ink.

Nagayama wrote in a skillful hand, "Three Hundred Thousand Yen. Genki Nagayama." He took a somewhat rumpled check from his breast pocket and pushed it together with the subscription book in Kazu's direction. "It's only a token," he said, "but tomorrow morning—it's the leaast I can do to atone for my sins—I'll squeeze all the money I can out of Yamanashi of the Imperial Bank. It wasn't because I disliked you, of course, that I did what I did . . . I'll telephone you tomorrow morning when I hear what Yamanashi has to say. I don't suppose you want me to call your house."

"Please telephone me at the Setsugoan."

"I'd like you to be ready to leave immediately if I call."

"Yes." Having said that, Kazu decided she would have to spend the night at the Setsugoan.

Late in the afternoon of the following day Kazu met the person she was to meet and accomplished all that she had to do. She returned then to her house in Koganei. She expected a rebuke from Noguchi, but her heart now was calm. Plans for the reopening of the Setsugoan were at length taking shape: the miracle had been accomplished.

The pampas grass on the Koganei Embankment shone white in the twilight. Overhead a flock of birds crossed the still bright sky. She recalled that this morning she had risen extremely early, too excited to sleep. When she strolled for the first time in months through the neglected garden of the Setsugoan, she heard the noise of wings as a swarm of little birds, resting on the slopes so thickly overgrown that weeds and grass were no longer distinguishable, flew up, startled at her approach. It was as if a single blow had shattered the glassy transparency of the morning air into a thousand fragments.

Kazu ordered the driver to stop the car beside the bridge, some distance this side of her house. She hesitated to have the car park alongside the gate. The driver opened the door, and she started to put out one foot, its white tabi sharply contrasting with the twilit road. Just at that moment, a man emerged from Noguchi's gate. She saw that he was coming her way. The figure approached unsteadily, with a brief case in one hand. His back was to the sunset and she could not see his face. He looked terribly old, and although his build was powerful, he stooped so badly that he seemed strengthless. The peaceful glow in the western sky seemed somehow to suggest the dying moments of idealism. The sun, sinking at the end of the fields, was lighting hundreds and thousands of candles, like some huge revolving lantern of empty ideals. The man walking with his back to the light was a silhouette pasted on the silk of the lantern, a shadow picture cut from a single sheet of thin black paper, which cast a dancing shadow on the silk. In that case, the man could only be Yamazaki.

Kazu reinstalled herself in the car. Lowering the window glass, she put out her head. The evening wind struck coldly against her face. She called Yamazaki by name when he was close enough so that she would not have to raise her voice. Startled even by this subdued voice, he looked up. "Oh, it's you, Mrs. Noguchi."

"Come in the car. I want to talk with you."

Yamazaki, clumsy as a bear, climbed into the car and sat beside Kazu.

"You'll be going directly back to Tokyo, won't you, Mr. Yamazaki?"

"Yes."

"Then why don't you use the car? I'm getting out here, and the car has to go back to town in any case."

"Much obliged. I'll do that then."

They sat in silence for a while inside the dark car. Then Kazu, looking straight ahead, asked, "What did you discuss with my husband?"

"Mr. Noguchi put his hands on the tatami, bowed to me, and said he was sorry. I've never seen him like that before. I must say, I was in tears."

Kazu's heart beat fast with foreboding. "What made him apologize to you?"

"Mr. Noguchi said, 'After all the trouble I've caused you since the election clearing up my personal affairs, Kazu has betrayed me. I'm down on my knees, and I'm asking your pardon. Please call off the negotiations.' "

"What negotiations?"

"Please don't pretend you don't know, Mrs. Noguchi. Breaking up the Setsugoan into lots, of course."

"What did he mean by saying I'd betrayed him?"

"He knows about the subscription book."

"Does he?" Kazu stared through the front window of the car into the darkness. The dim light at the gate of the Noguchi house fell on the road. A bare line of pale yellow was still visible in the darkening sky. The cherry trees on the embankment were masses of black shadows.

"Really, Mr. Yamazaki, I've caused you nothing but trouble," Kazu said after a pause.

"That's a strange thing to say. I haven't thought so myself particularly. I trust that in the future I may still look forward to the pleasure of your acquaintance."

"I'm happy to hear you say so, but there's no denying it, the trouble all started from my insistence on having my own way."

"I've known that all along." Yamazaki was coolly objective.

It occurred then to Kazu that, if only by way of acknowledgment of a year's friendship with Yamazaki, she should have informed him (if no one else) beforehand of the subscription book. But this secret belonged to a category quite apart from the world in which Yamazaki lived. On second thought, she had probably done right in not informing him.

"I'll be going now," Kazu said. She braced herself to rise from her seat, and in so doing her hand brushed against Yamazaki's on the seat beside her. His cold, silent hand crouched discontentedly in the dark.

Kazu's conscience bothered her, and at the same time she felt sorry for Yamazaki, left isolated. Aware that some bodily gesture would speak far better for her than words, she lay her hand over his and squeezed it hard. This had never happened before in their long acquaintance.

Yamazaki's eyes when he turned toward her in surprise glittered in the reflected light of the distant street lamps. He was not one, however, to misunderstand even so abrupt a gesture. It did not come as such a surprise that the resolution of the year since he first met Kazu at Noguchi's house should take this form. If this was not friendship, it was certainly not love. It was the self-indulgent relationship between two human beings, and since Yamazaki had hitherto preserved his objectivity by showing an unlimited tolerance, it could not be said that only Kazu was self-indulgent. In the end, like a painter destroying a carefully composed picture with the final stroke of his brush, Kazu had suddenly destroyed everything by her sudden, incongruous gesture of taking his hand. But Yamazaki, retreating to another angle, could easily forgive even such conduct, shallow in a lover and profanatory in a friend. His most vivid impression was of the strange power wrapped in Kazu's hand, soft and warm as a feather quilt. It was an illogical, ambiguous warmth that swept all before it, concealing strong destructive powers. It filled her flesh with its density, and this flesh had its own irreplaceable weight, heat, and darkness.

Kazu at last released his hand. "I'll say good-bye now . . . After all you went through I can certainly see why you'd feel pretty discouraged. My husband and I have been floundering around in much the same mood. Whatever we may do in the future . . ."

"Whenever you pass before a telegraph pole you'll remember the posters that were pasted there."

"Yes, that's right. It's unfortunate, but there are telegraph poles everywhere, even here in the backwoods."

This time Yamazaki disinterestedly patted the back of Kazu's hand. "It can't be helped. You'll recover by-and-by. Everybody feels the same way for a while after a party."

Kazu remembered the empty reflections of the gold screen in the main dining room of the Setsugoan after a banquet had ended.

When the red taillights of the car carrying Yamazaki

had receded into the distance, Kazu walked alone over the now completely darkened street toward her house. She wandered outside the gate for a while, unable to enter.

Finally, she made up her mind and went inside. She called to the maid in a deliberately loud voice. "Has the master finished his dinner?"

"No, ma'am. I'm preparing it now. Will you have your dinner too, Mrs. Noguchi?"

"Let me see. I'm not very hungry." Kazu paused. She could not picture herself and her husband sitting down together to dinner this evening. "I'll let you know later if I feel like eating."

Noguchi was in a room at the end of the house. Kazu called to him through the shoji, "I've just got back now."

There was no answer, but Kazu went in and sat down. Noguchi was reading a book. He did not so much as turn in Kazu's direction. She noticed first his head, almost completely white since the election, then the back seam of the kimono over his frail but erect shoulders. Noguchi, as always, wore his kimono awkwardly, and the seam was twisted to the left. His back, however, was extremely far removed; she knew that even if she had thought to straighten the seam, her hands could never reach it now.

"I've been informed of all your activities," Noguchi said after a while, his back still toward her. "Perhaps they were unavoidable as far as you were concerned, but I find them unpardonable. You've been unfaithful."

"What do you mean by that, please?" Her retort had a defiant ring. Noguchi was surprised at such forcefulness from Kazu, but he realized the next instant that there had been a simple verbal misunderstanding. He turned toward his wife for the first time and explained. Noguchi's voice showed no trace of agitation, and his words were calm, but she could sense somewhere a terrible fatigue which provided a curious contrast to the high-minded content of his remarks.

Noguchi believed that there was no room for divergence in human conduct, whether in politics or love. He was convinced that all human actions were based on the same principles, and that politics, love, and morality must, like the constellations, be governed by fixed laws. Thus, any one act of betrayal was exactly equal to the other acts of betrayal, and all were nothing less than betrayals of the fundamental principles as a whole. An adulteress's political chastity and a chaste woman's political betrayal represented the same kind of immorality. The worst crime was for an act of betrayal to spread infection to successive persons, thereby hastening a collapse of the entire structure of principles. According to this old-fashioned, Chinese-style political philosophy, Kazu's circulation of a subscription book among Noguchi's political enemies was tantamount to adultery: she had "slept" with these men.

Kazu listened distractedly to Noguchi's words. In the end, she knew, she would never understand these ideas. But she was scarcely less confident than Noguchi that her beliefs were ultimately correct.

The present incident had made Noguchi despair utterly of Kazu. He gave up any illusions about the possibility of correcting each of her transgressions. His extreme slowness in making this discovery spoke for the optimistic side of this upright man. Noguchi was so blinded by his own righteousness that he failed to perceive the essence of things. Why had he made Kazu his wife? Was it not perhaps because the deeper Noguchi believed in his principles, the more he unconsciously required this woman to desecrate them?

Noguchi was angry also because Kazu, though accommodating herself on the surface to his educational zeal, had not in fact responded sincerely to a single thing he taught her. Kazu, however, had completely failed to recognize in her husband's educational zeal anything stemming from fundamental beliefs; she could only suppose that his zeal was a mark of affection. It is generally impossible to educate and change a mature person, and when her husband's eyes shone, bewitched by this impossibility, she was right in interpreting this as a sign of affection. She had responded straightforwardly to this affection with a gentle submissiveness, having no choice but to get along as best she could with this logical passion for the impossible.

It was inconceivable that Noguchi could have failed to perceive Kazu's passion for things in constant motion, her fervor for activity, her innate love for rushing about, throwing herself completely into whatever she did. Kazu's attraction for him undoubtedly resided in these qualities, precisely the ones to arouse the pedagogical ardor of a conscientious man like Noguchi.

Noguchi required that Kazu faithfully obey his principles, but she was not so presumptuous as to hope that Noguchi would obey hers. Herein lay the loneliness implicit in her vitality: Kazu was hazily aware that she alone was capable of acting in accordance with her own principles. She possessed no logical passion of any kind. Logic merely chilled her. And it was this knowledge of the loneliness of her vitality that made Kazu always afraid of the loneliness after death.

Noguchi's next words, deliberately pronounced, were of course calculated to ignite these fears in Kazu. "Listen carefully. These are my final words. If you are willing to change your mind now, abandon your plans for reopening the Setsugoan, and sell the place, I am willing to pardon your almost unpardonable conduct, and to start again on a fresh footing . . . If you say 'Yes' now, you will barely make this last-minute reprieve. But if you say 'No' . . . I think you are fully aware of what that means, but I must ask you to remember that our relations will be at an end."

There flashed before Kazu's eyes an unvisited grave in some desolate cemetery, belonging to someone who had died without a family. This vision of the end of a life of solitary activity—a lonely, abandoned grave covered with weeds, leaning over, beginning to rot—sent a fathomless dark fear stabbing into Kazu's heart. If Kazu were no longer a member of the Noguchi family, she would assuredly travel a straight road leading to that desolate grave. This intuition of the future was insolently precise.

But something was calling Kazu from the distance. An animated life, every day wildly busy, many people coming and going—something like a perpetually blazing fire called her. That world held no resignation or abandoned hopes, no complicated principles; it was insincere and all its inhabitants fickle, but in return, drink and laughter bubbled up lightheartedly. That world seen from here looked like the torchlight of dancers scorching the night sky on a hilltop beyond dark meadows.

Kazu had no choice but to plunge in that direction, as her active energy commanded. Nothing, not even Kazu herself, could oppose its commands. And yet, Kazu's energy in the end would certainly lead her to a lonely, tumble-down, unattended grave.

Kazu shut her eyes.

It gave Noguchi an uneasy sensation to see his wife, sitting erect, her neckline straight, her eyes shut. He thought that he was all too well acquainted with this woman's incomprehensibility, but such an understanding was a hindrance: her present incomprehensibility was of an order entirely different from anything he had known before. He did not notice that Kazu was turning into a different woman.

Noguchi was thinking, "She's trying to discover some way to suit her own convenience again, no doubt about that. Her next step may be to persuade me with her tears. Whatever it is, I'm worn out by this woman. That's possibly a sign that I'm getting old, but as far as I'm concerned, exhaustion is the only accurate way to describe my feelings."

All the same, he was agitated by the childish expectancy and anxiety one feels in the moment of waiting before fireworks explode in the sky.

Noguchi had in this manner raised his final resolve into an airtight structure, and had driven Kazu inside. The course of events which led to Kazu's being forced into choosing between two alternatives had, however, been initiated by Kazu herself, and one might more properly say that Noguchi had erected this stockade without a loophole, not precisely against his will, but out of a kind of weariness. He felt that whichever answer Kazu made would be all right with him.

Noguchi dreaded most Kazu's next, not unlikely change of heart, and the bother any shift would entail. On the surface he showed an adolescent fretfulness, but he yearned now to settle in some permanent fashion, at the first possible moment, the few remaining years left him. He had no further inclination for repairs, rebuilding, modifications in the blueprints, or recasting of plans. His mind and flesh were incapable now of enduring any uncertainties. Quivering like a piece of fruit inside a dish of jello, he waited impatiently for the moment when the gelatine would kindly harden. It seemed to him that the coagulation of the world would have to be completed before he could look up to the blue sky with an easy mind and admire to his heart's content the sunrise and sunset and the rustling of the treetops.

Noguchi, like many other retired politicians, had wished to save "poetry" for his declining years. He had never had the leisure to appreciate that desiccated storage food, nor did he expect that it would taste good, but to such men as Noguchi, poetry lay hidden not in poetry itself so much as in an untroubled craving for poetry; poetry in fact symbolized the unshakable stability of the world. Poetry would make its appearance—indeed, would have to appear—when there was no further danger of the world changing, when one knew that there would be no further assaults of uncertainty, hopes, or ambitions.

At such a time, he expected, the moral constraint of a lifetime and the armor of logic would melt and dissolve into poetry, like a column of white smoke rising in the autumn sky. But when it came to the poetry of security, Kazu was his senior, and she knew much better than he its ineffectuality.

Noguchi did not realize that he would never love nature. If he could have loved nature he would assuredly have loved Kazu more expertly. During his walk he had taken pleasure in the last traces of old Japan visible in the

Koganei area, supposing them to be the beauty of nature, but the aged cherry trees, the towering elms, the clouds, the evening sky had been no more than the idealized self-portrait his honest clumsiness had painted.

Kazu's eyes were still shut.

At this instant Noguchi felt utter bafflement at the prospect of being trapped within a domestic life of eternally renewed instability. He was sure that even if he put his hand on Kazu's shoulder and shook her, she would not budge, that she had solidified on the spot and would go on sitting there. And perhaps the months and years until he died would pass in stagnation, and the world would coagulate, not as he had expected, but in this weird form.

Kazu slowly opened her eyes.

While her eyes were shut her mind had resolutely crossed the mountain, and she had reached the only answer possible for her. She had immersed herself in the darkness of her closed lids and—perhaps now for the first time completely under her husband's influence—she answered as never before with perfect logic. "I'm sorry, there's no other way. I intend to reopen the Setsugoan. I intend to pay back the money I borrowed if I have to work the flesh from my bones."

Noguchi was suddenly filled with terrible hatred for Kazu. He had spent the whole of the previous night in a rage, but today, since seeing Yamazaki and then Kazu, his rage had entirely subsided, and he had been able to act with an indifferent, cold resignation. He had not foreseen the hatred that suddenly welled up within him when he heard Kazu choose with dignity one of the two alternatives he had forced on her.

Which answer had Noguchi expected? Would he have hated her less if she had chosen the other alternative?

In any case, when he struck her in displeasure over her irresponsible actions during the campaign, he had not been so upset as now, when Kazu had evidently stolen his own weapon of logic, and become his enemy fair and square.

Unlike previous occasions, Kazu had not shed a single

tear. Her fair-skinned face actually seemed cheerful, and her ample figure, sitting perfectly erect, had the exquisite poise of a finely carved doll.

Kazu looked into Noguchi's eyes; one glance and she perceived the hatred blazing in the old man's thin, dignified frame. This was by no means the expression of the educator, nor was it the admonitory look in the eyes of the hard-to-please stoical father . . . Kazu, seeing it, trembled with joy.

Not a sound could be heard from the world outside the tightly shut shoji. The lights in the room seemed suddenly to brighten: Noguchi's simple bookshelves and desk, the scissors on his desk, the paint on the few articles of furniture, shone and seemed to stand out in more detailed relief than usual. The new tatami gave off a grassy fragrance.

They stared at each other for a long while. This was the first time Kazu had been able to look squarely into her husband's eyes in this way. Noguchi's shoulders twitched with anger; his whole body loathed Kazu. She feared that he might collapse on the spot.

Then she became genuinely afraid. She considered one way and another to look after him. But she was too far removed for her hand to reach him; the strength which only Kazu now possessed to soothe Noguchi's chagrin was no longer for him. The same was true of Noguchi. Although his hatred was bit by bit subsiding, he knew that only makeshift expedients were left. From the moment that Kazu made her answer, his fist would no longer reach her body. Ludicrous as it may seem, a kind of courtesy now restrained his hand. This courtesy made Kazu feel as if a damp shroud were being wrapped around her body.

After a long silence Noguchi said finally, "That's your decision, is it? In that case, I intend to start divorce proceedings. You have no objection, I take it."

CHAPTER XIX

BEFORE THE BANQUET

By mutual consent Noguchi struck Kazu's name from the family register. Kazu gathered together her belongings and returned to the Setsugoan. When rumors of these events got around, the former employees of the Setsugoan, who had scattered in all directions when the place closed, reappeared one after another to request that they be taken back. Kazu's eyes filled with tears of joy.

The house itself was run down, but the garden was a wilderness. The former gardener came with several young assistants, and announced that by way of celebrating the reopening, he was offering his services gratis. He undertook to restore the garden as quickly as possible to its former condition.

Whenever she had a moment's leisure, Kazu delighted in going down into the garden to watch the gardeners at their daylong labors of mowing the lawn and pruning the shrubbery. At night owls hooted, and by day she saw the trim silhouettes of the kites which built their nest at the top of the tallest pine. Sometimes, as the weeds were being cut down, a small pheasant would scurry off toward the far end of the garden. The elder tree which had been allowed to spread unhindered, was dotted with purple fruits, but still kept a few faded summer blossoms whose fragrance hovered faintly like some ghostly presence. The hedge of *dodan* bushes, the leaves now most brilliantly tinted, cast lovely shadows by the old gate at the entrance.

Kazu, watching the garden take on day by day more of its former beauty, could not feel that the image gradually emerging like a thermotype was the same garden she had known. It certainly looked the same, but it was not the garden that Kazu had once treasured in her mind like a precisely drawn map that she had memorized and cupped in the palms of her hands. The transparent garden she had known to the last corner was lost. Each tree, each stone, in its proper place, corresponded perfectly with Kazu's carefully arranged catalogue of the known human emotions, but this correspondence was now lost.

The grass was mowed and rolled. The branches which had intricately multiplied were lopped down and the sky brightened. The gradually emerging face of the garden was as beautiful as a woman gently waking from sleep and shadowy dreams, and its features were remarkably similar to those she had known, but for Kazu not one dot, one stroke, belonged to the known world.

One day it rained and the gardener took the day off. The weather cleared toward evening, and the island in the pond, its thick growth of bamboo grass, and the water of the pond sparkled in the sunlight. The uncertain scattered light flickered across the pond, and the garden seemed to Kazu to express an uncanny joy she had never known. Again, on another morning the garden was enveloped in mist, and the pines thrusting their branches through the mist seemed to be surrendering themselves to some kind of unpleasant memories.

Around this time Yamazaki sent an answer to the long letter Kazu had written him. She went into the garden that morning, thinking she would read the letter in the lingering, Indian summer warmth.

The southeast pond glittered in the sun, and the sedate dark green of a huge ilex tree at the center, surrounded by old imposing pines, chestnuts, nettle trees, and oaks, marked the exact apex of the wood in the background. The stone lantern, the focal point of the broad expanse of lawn, alone benefiting from the long closure of the Setsugoan, had gained an antique repose; when the area around it was carefully weeded, it stood out more prominently and vividly than ever. The sky was clear today, and fine cirrus clouds drifted between the treetops.

The garden, once folded up so small, had swelled like a

paper flower in water and had become a vast park filled with riddles and mysteries. In it plants and birds pursued their quiet occupations unmolested. The garden was full of things Kazu knew nothing of; each day she brought back one from the garden and, little by little making it her own, she would grind it in a small mortar ... She tried rubbing it in her palms, her fingers, as she might rub a medicine, but the garden's hoard of fresh, unknown ingredients was limitless, and would probably enrich Kazu's fingers inexhaustibly.

Kazu, stepping through the stripes of sunlight filtering through the trees, walked to a bench by the path, sat, and began to read Yamazaki's letter.

Thank you for your letter and invitation to the banquet celebrating the reopening of the Setsugoan. It may not seem entirely appropriate for me to offer congratulations, but forgetting my position for the moment, I should like to express my heartfelt best wishes.

Your letter did not touch in the least on the recent unfortunate events, but was concerned exclusively with an account of how the garden is being readied for the reopening. I believe that I can imagine what prompted you to write in that way.

When I think how in the past couple of years your confidence in your knowledge of people has been shattered, how you have obtained in place of peace of mind only uncertainty, and in place of happiness a new, painful knowledge, how when you tried to love you learned recognition, how you ended at the place where you thought you would begin, and began at the place you had ended ... how you have been able to secure your present, peaceful uncertainty by sacrificing everything, my nature is such that I feel less sympathy than respect.

When I look back now, I think perhaps you might have been able to enjoy happiness had it not been for the election. Mr. Noguchi might have been happy too. But it now seems to me that the election cannot be said to have been a misfortune in a real sense, for it smashed every kind of counterfeit happiness and resulted in you and Mr. Noguchi showing each other your naked selves. I have been wallowing in the bog of politics for a long time, and I have in fact come to be quite fond of it. In it corruption cleanses people, hyprocrisy reveals human character more than half-hearted honesty, and vice may, at least for a moment, revive a helpless trust . . . Just as when you throw laundry into a centrifugal dryer, it rotates so fast that the shirt or underwear you've just thrown in vanishes before your eyes, what we normally call human nature instantly disappears in the whirlpool of politics. I like its fierce operation. It doesn't necessarily purify, but it makes you forget what should be forgotten, and overlook what should be overlooked. It works a kind of inorganic intoxication. That is why, no matter how badly I fail, no matter what disastrous experiences I encounter, I shall never leave politics as long as I live.

You were probably right in returning to warm blood and a human vitality, and Mr. Noguchi right too in returning to lofty ideals and beautiful principles. It may seem cruel of me to say it, but in the eyes of an outsider, everything has found its place, the birds have all returned to their nests.

This winter seems unusually warm, but I hope that you will please not neglect your health. After all the terrible mental and physical exhaustion you have experienced, you will be kept very busy now by your work at the Setsugoan. The pressure of work will undoubtedly serve to distract you, but I hope that you will be as careful as possible about your health.

I shall be delighted to be present on the night of the reopening.